Following in HIS Steps

Part 1: Starting Out on the Right Foot

Student Edition (Teen & Adult)

A Life-Changing, Foundational Bible
Course for New and Maturing Believers

Joy W. Estes

Foreword by

Dr. Robert A. Dickard

WESTBOW
PRESS®
A DIVISION OF THOMAS NELSON
& ZONDERVAN

WestBow Press books may be ordered through booksellers or by contacting:

WestBow Press
A Division of Thomas Nelson & Zondervan
1663 Liberty Drive
Bloomington, IN 47403
www.westbowpress.com
1 (866) 928-1240

ISBN: 978-1-5127-9405-2 (sc)
ISBN: 978-1-5127-9404-5 (e)

Library of Congress Control Number: 2017910048

Print information available on the last page.

WestBow Press rev. date: 11/2/2017

If this book is lost, please return to:
Name: _____
Address _____
City/St./Zip _____
Phone: _____

This book was given to me by:
Name: _____
Address: _____
City/St/Zip: _____
Phone: _____

Write a friend's name below whom I will recite memorization to each week.
Friend's name: _____
Phone: _____
E-mail: _____
Street Address: _____
City/ State/ Zip _____

****

~ ~ ~

Dedicated first to our wonderful Lord and Savior Jesus Christ, Who saved us out of darkness and into His marvelous light! May our Lord Jesus Christ receive all honor and glory for His inspiration and guidance to produce this course for the children in His family.

~ ~ ~

Next, I also dedicate this course to my wonderful family, who gave me advice and support and sacrificed their time with me so God could lead me in writing this course.

~ ~ ~

Third, this curriculum is dedicated to my late parents, Rev. Dewey and Mary Weaver, who consistently loved God and me and reared me up with a godly influence. They left a spiritual heritage worth more than gold and taught by example so God's Word could be applied personally. This helped me know how to experience real life as God intended, then to influence others in God's Word in order to impact lives for eternity.

~ ~ ~

I am very thankful for the professional editing by Dr. Sarah Bell. I am also grateful for the extra reviews I received from Lisa Boozer, Dr. Tim Harris, Dr. Wayne Milam, Shaneeka Minniefield, and Oscar and Susan Thorsland.

Following in HIS Steps is a two-book set containing Parts 1 and 2. This book contains only *Part 1: Starting Out on the Right Foot*, Chapters 1 through 6. The second book in the set is *Part 2: Walking in the Light*, Chapters 1 through 6 (coming soon). *Part 1: Starting Out on the Right Foot* (6 week course) is meant to be sold with *Part 2: Walking in the Light* (6 week course) as a complete 12 week course. See ordering information below.

For more <u>books</u>, contact: Westbow Press
<u>www.westbowpress.com</u> or call 1 (866) 928-1240

For <u>Leader Guides and the Reproducer CD program</u> that go with this book, contact:
Real Life Impact Ministries, Inc.
P.O. Box 397
Toccoa, Georgia 30577
E-mail: <u>reallifeimpact@gmail.com</u>
The best way to order the extra items is through our website:
<u>www.reallifeimpactministries.com</u>

Following in HIS Steps
Part 1: Starting Out on the Right Foot
By: Joy W. Estes
Printed in the USA
© Copyright 2017
All rights reserved.

Contents

Chapter 1: The New Birth Story

Chapter 2: The Evidences of God's Gift

Chapter 3: Look at My Picture - Who I Am in Christ

Chapter 4: Birthday Gifts – What I Have in Christ

What Others are Saying about *Following in HIS Steps*

Joy Estes has skillfully drawn from her and her husband Doug's many years of experience in mentoring believers. *Following in HIS Steps* is a practical, systematic Bible study that is solid in biblical doctrine, engaging, and challenging for those who are serious about their Christian growth. Commonsensical illustrations drive home truths with ease. It is a refreshing and profitable study.

Dr. Wayne Milam, Pastor / Marriage and Family Counselor

In a market crowded with materials for making disciples, *Following in HIS Steps* stands out…. Joy Estes offers a comprehensive, yet accessible method for discipling both new believers and seasoned Christians alike. In *Following in HIS Steps*, she instructs students in foundational truths that will provide a foundation for a lifetime walk with Christ.

Dr. Timothy Harris, Senior Pastor / East Side Baptist Church / Liberty, SC

I have read *Following in HIS Steps* by Joy Estes. It is an excellent resource for the beginning believer. It provides clear and detailed steps that all believers must take to "grow in grace and in the knowledge of our Lord and Savior." It is not only a valuable resource for the beginning Christian; it will also prove to be a great refresher manual for the seasoned believer. *Following in HIS Steps* is clearly written with great examples that will challenge believers to be more productive as they strive to serve our Lord Jesus Christ more effectively.

Mr. Oscar Thorsland, Retired High School Principal

We both went through the course and feel it would be very beneficial to new and maturing Christians alike. We also had an opportunity to help with skits and listen to people learn the verses. We learned a lot ourselves. Highly recommend to anyone that wants to learn more about our Lord and His Word!

Mr. Randy Mullikin, Deacon and *Mrs. Ann Mullikin*, Sunday School Teacher

I felt this Bible study was really helpful to understand how to start doing devotions on my own and what I was supposed to do. I learned that it is very important to stay in the Word and study it because that is how we learn more about Him and how we should live.

Miss Brianna Vaughn, Teen Student

My husband and I took this class several years ago. What I remember most is that Doug and Joy saw something in my written testimony that prompted them to explain the lordship of Christ over my life. For the first time, I understood how essential it was to my relationship with God and my spiritual growth! It was key for me, and I'm so grateful for this class!

Mrs. Leanne Bell, Stay-at-Home Mom

I studied *Following in HIS Steps* with my husband in 2015. We both enjoyed the program very much. The weekly Bible verses challenged us as well as made us want to keep studying the chapters. We both felt that we grew together in our faith and were spiritually stronger for taking the class. I would highly recommend this study.

Mrs. Diana Watson, Nurse

How This Bible Study can be Used in Your Life

This book is intended for new Christians and maturing believers. <u>It comes with a separate Leader Guide</u> and other resources for the teacher/facilitator to lead in each six-week course. If you are reading this in an E-book form, you will need to fill in the blanks on the e-book. **You can use this Bible study book in:**

- **Churches:**
  - New Christian class
  - New Member class
  - Use with the "Reproducer Plan©" to Help Grow your Church
  - Volunteer and Leader Training
  - Foundational class for all Church Members
  - Specialized classes, as in Ladies Bible studies
  - Community Outreach Bible studies
  - Teen or Adult Bible study and Memorization courses
  - Offer with AWANA or other programs
- **Christian school Bible courses**
- **Home school Bible studies**
- **Small-group Bible studies**
- **One-on-One Discipleship**
- **Individual or Family Devotions**

How can *Following in HIS Steps* help you in your Christian life? First, I want to assure you that this is no ordinary Bible study. It is a hands-on way of connecting intimately with God so you can start learning to live the way Jesus meant for you to live: abundantly! By completing Part 1 of this course, you will not only grow in knowledge, but your whole life can be transformed by learning to live your life God's way. By fully participating in both books with this course, you will:

* Practice spending time with God each day
* Memorize Bible verses and the 66 books of the Bible
* Discover the foundations of the Christian life
* Serve God with the spiritual gifts He has given you
* Follow God's great plan and purpose for your life

* Be prepared to share your faith
* Know what you believe and why
* Practice wise habits
* Discover who you are in Christ
* Learn blessings you have in God

* Discover how committing to God and His Word will change your life
* Learn how to disciple a new believer in Christ and so much more!

Dear Family Member in Christ,

Whether you have recently become a believer or you have been saved for many years, I am excited for you! You made the wisest choice anyone could ever make when you chose to become part of God's family. This means we are spiritual brothers and sisters in the family of God. Now that you have started out on the right foot with Jesus as your personal Lord and Savior, God has rescued you from the punishment for your sin. He has set your feet on the Rock: Jesus Christ! Yes, Jesus is your true foundation. God's Word says, "He also brought me up out of a horrible pit, out of the miry clay, and set my feet upon a rock, and established my steps" (Psalm 40:2).

My prayer is that this Bible study will help you grow in your love relationship with Jesus Christ and follow in His steps just as a young child would follow in his father's steps. By committing to the study of God's Word, He will steer you toward the wonderful plan He has for your life. It says in Psalm 119:133, "Direct my steps by Your word, and let no iniquity have dominion over me." Just as a newborn baby needs milk to grow, so you need the spiritual nourishment from the Bible to help you mature and experience the abundant life as a child of God. So grab a Bible and follow along as you start on the most exciting adventure of your life!

All for Jesus,

Joy

Foreword

I remember hearing Delos Miles, my Evangelism professor in seminary, say something like this: "Evangelism without discipleship is not real evangelism." Evangelism and discipleship are two sides of the same coin. One of the reasons there is a huge dropout rate of those who have professed faith in Christ might be because there has been no significant discipleship in their life.

One of the primary functions of the church, as seen in Acts 2, is discipleship. The definition of *discipleship* is giving baby Christians the opportunity to become the person God saved them to be. Jesus calls us to follow Him in loving obedience to His teachings. It is imperative for new Believers to learn to study the Bible and to develop a personal devotional life. Those who have been Christians for years need to be challenged to develop a deep prayer life, to nurture others, and to share the faith and to pass it on to those who will be the next generation of Believers.

I am grateful that God has used Joy Estes to write this textbook on discipleship. It is my prayer and belief that He will use this tool to grow His people into strong, healthy, mature Believers who are equipped to be salt and light in this generation. In this book, Joy provides the tools for a church, small group, or class to "go deep in order to grow strong." As one who has poured her life into the church, she has a great desire to see Christians grow in the Lord. She understands how Christians sometimes struggle in their walk. Because she has a love for the Word of God, all her lessons are faithful and true to the Scriptures.

I recommend this book to anyone of any age who wants to be more than a Sunday Christian. For one who desires to learn to walk in the Spirit and to go from milk to the meat of the Word, this material will be invaluable.

Dr. Robert A. Dickard
Director of Missions
Piedmont Baptist Association

Introduction

When you start on a journey, you need to know where you are going and how to get there, so it is important to read this introduction before starting on the daily Bible study devotions. May God bless you as you start out on the right foot and follow in His steps on your journey with Him.

1. For New and Maturing Believers
2. How to Get the Most from This Bible Study
3. Goals of this Bible Study
4. Bible Study Topics

For New and Mature Believers

This Bible study is for all kinds of people. If you are a new believer or have been a Christian for many years, read below to see how this course can apply to your life.

- If you are a New Believer (one who has recently accepted Jesus Christ as personal Savior and Lord or one who desires to grow stronger), this Bible study (Parts 1 and 2) provides the essential foundational truths and practical living advice to help you start to succeed in your Christian life. This will enable you to learn enough right away to know how to make wise decisions before you get discouraged and tricked by the ungodly philosophies of this world. If Christians do not study God's Word and get around godly, wise people, then the next verse could come true which says, "My people are destroyed for lack of knowledge" (Hosea 4:6). But that will not happen if you continue seeking God and the study of His Word. 1 Peter 2:2 says, "As newborn babes, desire the pure milk of the word, that you may grow thereby." This study starts with the basics and leads you into a deeper study as you continue to be committed each week and to each level. Just as a baby starts with milk and eventually graduates to meat, you will start with the milk (basics) of the Word and soon understand the meat, that is, have answers to the deeper questions in life. Then you will not be destroyed by your lack of knowledge of God's success principles; instead, you will be able to experience the abundant life as you study God's plan for your life through His Word.

- If you are a Maturing Believer (one who has accepted Jesus as personal Savior and Lord many years ago and one who has some knowledge of God's Word and has some success as a Christian), this course will strengthen your spiritual walk toward more victory and joy and guide you in discipling others in the Lord. We all have gaps in our spiritual journey. There is knowledge we have not learned or applied from God's Word. This course is meant to fill in those gaps as you complete each week's daily devotions and in all the levels. It will help give you a more solid foundation so God can make you stronger in knowing Him more intimately, obeying, having victory, evangelizing, and making disciples of others (using this book). Then you can start experiencing the real, abundant life—making an impact on our world! As you go through this course, look at it from the perspective of how you can gain more ideas and knowledge for a sure foundation that better equips you to love, obey, serve God, and disciple another believer. Whether you have been saved for a few days or many years, you can live more successfully by learning to apply Biblical principles that help you reach your potential in Christ.

How to Get the Most from this Bible Study

- <u>Personal Bible study</u>: If you are using this book for personal devotions and memorization, it will be very beneficial. If so, we suggest that you find an accountability partner to listen to your memory work. Then ask a church staff member or church leader to read and make suggestions on your testimony sheet and spiritual gifts profile. This person can help you figure out where to use your spiritual gifts as well. If you can have your church staff member sign that he or she checked these areas off for you and email us, we will email your church a certificate to give you. Continue reading the instructions in this section.

- <u>Bible study with a weekly class through church</u>: This course is meant to be used best under the spiritual guidance and instruction of an experienced Bible teacher and assistants in a weekly class for ages 12 to 100. Although you can still benefit from completing this course on your own, you will learn much more when you have a Bible teacher and others holding you accountable to complete the course. You will benefit tremendously through the encouragement, wisdom, and discernment of others who have already lived through the challenges of the Christian life and experienced victories. When you attend this weekly Bible study, it helps you finish what you start, therefore ensuring success in this course, and starting out on the right foot in your spiritual life.

- <u>Personal Bible study and a weekly class through church</u>: As you use the Bible version of your choice and complete the six days of Bible devotions each week, there are written questions to think about from the Bible verses it tells you to read. If you are not sure how to look up Bible verses, see Appendix A or ask your Bible study leader. If you see an *a* or *b* after a verse reference, *a* means it is only the first part of the verse and *b* means it is only the second part of the verse. How will you know if you get the right answers after you look up the Bible verses? First, read the Bible verse. Next, think about what it means. Ask God to help you understand it. Then write your answer down. You are not graded unless you are in school. Writing answers will help you think about God's Word and apply it to your life. <u>Check to see if your answer is on target by seeing the answers in *italics* in the paragraph following each question.</u> Do not be discouraged if you do not have the exact word; just check for the meaning. But do not cheat yourself and just write down the *italics* answers. You will not get as much out of it if you do not think for yourself.

- **Plan to be faithful in attending the lesson at your church each week.** Attending this course needs to become a <u>priority</u> in your life and that of your family. Each week is a crucial and important piece of the puzzle that will come together as a beautiful picture as you are committed to finish it. This commitment is essential in building a strong spiritual foundation and in reaching your potential. This will result in God truly blessing your life and those you will influence as He wants to. You will learn how to develop God's wonderful plan and purpose for your life. This book is the path that can start you on that plan! 1 Corinthians 4:2 says, "Moreover it is required in stewards that one be found faithful." God expects you to be faithful to Him, worshipping Him daily, and attending church and Sunday school (small group Bible studies) each week. Once you start, stick to it to get the most from it. We cheat ourselves out of blessings when we are not faithful. After all, God has always been faithful to us and will continue to be so. When you decide you will be loyal, God will bless you for your commitment.

1. <u>Do your best to plan trips out of town so you can be back in time for this course</u>. Some trips because of work are unavoidable, but other trips can be scheduled so you can be back in time for this Bible study. We know that vacations or ministry opportunities will need to happen with families, especially in the summer. So when you <u>have</u> to miss a class, make sure you take the daily devotions with you so you can still learn the material. Keep in contact with your accountability partner too.

2. <u>Go to bed at a decent hour the night before this study</u>. This helps you to feel better and be more alert and disciplined the next day. If another member of your family is taking this course and decides not to attend some time, make sure you are committed and disciplined anyway. Remember, **you become whatever you are committed to do.** Do not let others drag you down or rob you of your growth or joy in the Lord.

3. <u>Be prepared. The devil will throw problems in your way</u>. Just realize it is the enemy trying to distract you from your faithful commitment and from God's best plan in your life. Do not give in! Remember this: the one time you miss attending this Bible study is usually the time God had the greatest blessing for you, or when He would have answered a problem or need in your life, or you would have learned something that you could have used to help someone else. Putting God first by faithful attendance will always result in added blessings and stronger growth.

4. <u>It takes discipline to finish strong in this race</u>. 1 Cor. 9:27 says, "But I discipline my body and bring it into subjection, lest, when I have preached to others, I myself should become disqualified." Just as Olympic participants finish strong only when they persevere, so you will finish strong with rewards only when you have the discipline to finish what you start. 2 Tim. 4:7 says "I have fought the good fight, I have finished the race, I have kept the faith." Doing these things will ensure that you will "Start Out on the Right Foot" in the race of the Christian life, beginning with this course.

•   **Come prepared by bringing your Bible, pen, and daily devotions with you to the Bible study.** Being prepared with your materials will ensure that you are more likely to reach your potential and develop a solid foundation in God's family. Our family has a habit of putting materials we are taking with us by the door the night before. We can't forget it; otherwise we would trip over it. Whatever you do to remember your Bible, this book and a pen, it will aid you in your growth during this study.

- **Plan to be 15 minutes early and you will be on time.** The devil will fight you in attending this Bible study because it is against his plan for your destruction. God wants to bless you and your family through this Bible study, but also many more people for eternity that you will influence as a result. Plan for distractions and delays so you can be on time and not miss out on anything God wants to show you. <u>The beginning part of class is very crucial.</u> There may be prayer requests, important announcements, an accountability time, an interesting media introduction, possibly a gift drawing, and a fellowship or game time to build stronger friendships. We all need to encourage one another. So think of others and how you can help the ones attending this course. Then God will bless you in ways you could never imagine.

- **Come prepared to participate by taking notes and entering in on the discussion.** No one will make you speak in front of anyone. But this course is intended to build godly friendships where we can all learn from one another. You have been through a variety of experiences and learned lessons that are different from those of other people. We each have input that can help someone else.

- **Be faithful in spending daily time with God through the devotions provided that go along with these lessons.** The home studies are planned to be used with the teacher's weekly comments and will not have the same value apart from your completing them each day. <u>You will receive ten times more out of this study by completing the personal Bible study time instead of just being fed each week.</u> If you just attend these Bible study meetings each week, you will be blessed and have questions answered as well as having new insights revealed. But if you are actively involved in completing the Bible studies and memorization each day, you will receive 95% more blessing and growth! Someone has said, "Telling isn't teaching… listening isn't learning… you learn to do by doing."

Spending time with God in His Word may be a new habit for you, but do not give up. (1) Choose a <u>time</u> (15 minutes in the morning and 15 minutes later in the day or at night). (2) Choose a <u>place</u> free from distractions so you can finish each day of the devotions. Remember it is a process of growth. Just as a toddler learns to walk only as he keeps getting up when he falls down, so you will learn to spiritually walk with God only as you determine not to give up. You will enjoy learning and listening to the Lord Jesus each day as He speaks to you personally through the Bible studies and through prayer. You can also bring so much more to your Bible study group to help others when you are prepared. It is not hard when it becomes a habit. Just as exercise is hard at first, but once you get started, it becomes a little easier and you are encouraged when you see the physical results. So you will see spiritual results through changes in your life as you commit to be faithful to complete these daily devotions with God.

- **Remember to memorize the verses given to you each week.** Hiding God's Word in your heart ensures that you will not sin against Him. "Your word I have hidden in my heart, that I might not sin against You" (Psalm 119:11). There are easy ways to memorize Scripture that you will learn in class and at the end of this book. If you want to receive true joy and victory, then be accountable to a friend in your church or school group to memorize the Scripture each week.

- **Be willing to participate as an accountability partner/friend/spiritual brother or sister in the Lord.** If you are willing to help others, God will bless you in great ways. You also need to be willing to let others hold you accountable. This is <u>not</u> about condemning each other, but instead encouraging one another in love each week. A quote says it best: "Coming together is a start; keeping together is progress; working together is success."[1]

- **Think of how you can apply each lesson to your own life each week, and then pass on these truths, principles, or useful suggestions that you receive.** In this way, you will learn to make practical use of them and also invest your life in others. You do not want to waste your time, right? This is not another course in which you just get more knowledge. Instead, it is designed to be a life-changing course as a result of <u>doing, participating, committing, and applying</u> what you learn to your life. Get ready. The devil will try to fight you. He will throw temptations in your way through circumstances and even through well-meaning people. The Bible says, "A faithful man will abound with blessings" (Proverbs 28:20a). Do you want your life to change for the better? Then be faithful! It also says, "I can do all things through Christ who strengthens me" (Philippians 4:13). You can do it! Enjoy this exciting, life-changing adventure starting right now. Are you ready to produce a "Real Life Impact" in your life and in others' lives? Let's get started.

Goals for the *Following in HIS Steps* Course, Books 1 and 2

- Learn to have **consistent devotions**, loving and knowing God deeper, excited to meet Him every morning.

- Develop a solid foundation, knowing **what you believe and why** and **who you are in Christ** with God's Word as the foundation for all your decisions.

- **Experience victory over wrong habits**, living the abundant life in Christ with others as accountability partners, also developing godly friendships.

- **Become more committed to God, family, church, and small group Bible study** and have the right priorities in God's order.

- Get to know My Father **God's attributes** and choose to **make Jesus Lord** out of a love commitment to obey God in all areas.

- Study how to be **wise in decision-making,** discerning **God's purpose and plan** for your life; grow to love all kinds of people and **witness to others with confidence,** with practice opportunities provided in this course.

- Become a **memorizer of God's Word** and learn to **form successful habits** that affect every area of your life.

- Discover how to **disciple those you lead to the Lord** using this course to help you equip others to evangelize and disciple, reproducing and multiplying yourself for God's kingdom.

- Find out and use your **spiritual gifts** by getting involved in service to God as a lifestyle through your church. Also **learn the treasures in God's Word and secrets to prayer.**

- Learn how to **view problems as opportunities** for God's power to be shown in your life: for character to be developed, joy to be revealed, and life lessons that steer you toward **becoming better instead of bitter.**

- Grow to become **a person of integrity** with God's standards and convictions for successful living, developing a blameless testimony.

- **Discover how to have healthy relationships**, living out God's best plan and purpose in my life, making right choices that lead to living in a functional family that pleases God. Strong families strengthen the church and our Christian influence on our world.

CHAPTER 1
The New Birth Story

DAY 1
Unending True Love

See the Introduction section for instructions on how to make this Bible study a success for you. The section below will be at the beginning of each day of your Bible study and will contain the memorization portion. It is important you remember to read the memory verses, references, and Gospel points (GP) five times each before starting your Bible study each day. Or you can choose to play a memory game and memorize faster. (See Appendix B for memory game ideas.) It only takes a few minutes to read the memory work five times but this will help you memorize everything by the end of each week. The verses in this book will help prepare you to know what you believe, be ready to share your faith, be encouraged and more victorious in your Christian walk, and so much more! Enjoy your new adventure in God's Word!

<u>**Memory Verses and Gospel Points (GP):**</u>

1. <u>**GP1:**</u> God loves you! (John 3:16; Jeremiah 31:3)
   <u>**John 3:16**</u> "For God so loved the world that He gave His only begotten Son, that whoever believes in Him should not perish, but have everlasting life."

2. <u>**GP2**</u>: All have sinned. (Romans 3:23, 5:8, 6:23; Luke 13:3; Ephesians 2:8-9)
   <u>**Romans 3:23**</u> "For all have sinned and fall short of the glory of God."

3. <u>**Romans 5:8**</u> "But God demonstrates His own love toward us, in that while we were still sinners, Christ died for us."

Lord Jesus, please prepare my heart and mind to understand and apply Your Word to my life today. Show me something new this week that can help me in my Christian walk and that I can use to encourage another person. In Jesus' name, Amen.

What is your new birth story that tells how you became a child in God's family? There are many terms used to describe a child of God, such as "saved," "born again," "Christian," "Jesus is my Savior," "personally accepted," "believer," "redeemed," and "salvation." Can you truly know for sure you are a child of God who will spend eternity in heaven, not hell? Let's start with the evidence and think about it this way: If you were in a country that did not believe in the true God or honor Him, would the change in your life prove that you are a real believer? Let's imagine you are in a court of law in that nation. Is there enough evidence to convict you of being a Christian? Write down all the evidence about yourself that you would share in a court of law to prove that you are really a true Christian. Write down everything that describes you, positive and negative: _____

Do you think your testimony of confirming facts would prove you are a child of God?_____

To be clear, good works do not take away any sin, nor will they make you a Christian. Read **Ephesians 2:8-9**. Write two words that tell how you are saved from the punishment of your sin. _____ _____ God has *grace* (undeserved favor) for you and is willing to give you the precious gift of being saved. Salvation is a gift when you accept it by *faith* in God's work on the cross to pay for your sins, and believe in His resurrection. You are not putting any faith in any of your works on earth. But what role do your good works play in showing that you are truly God's child?

Read **Matthew 7:15-23**. In this passage, what is the one word that tells us when a person is a real Christian or not? (vs. 17) _____ When you have been saved by God's grace and your faith in Christ's finished work on the cross, then your life will change. You will display the *fruit* of good works after your salvation. Is there a change in you? _____

Is everyone who calls on the Lord's name, who goes to church, and does good works really saved? _____ Who then is really a child of God? (See vs. 21.) _____ Now some people can fake it on the outside by doing lots of good works, serving in church, and helping lots of people. But God knows those *who are obedient to His will*, who have the desire in their heart to please the Lord more than themselves. He knows those who have pure motives and are not doing good works out of guilt or to look good in front of others.

Your salvation will <u>not</u> be judged based on your works, but whether you are in Jesus Christ. After being saved, your name is in the Lamb's Book of Life. That is all that determines your fate. But if you are truly God's child, you will have a changed life! Your life will have an overflow that produces good works out of love for God. But good deeds alone are not enough evidence to prove you are going to heaven. The two Judgments will reveal the truth about each one of us.

All Christians will stand before God someday at the Judgment Seat of Christ and receive rewards for their good works done for the Lord Jesus. (See 2 Corinthians 5:10 and Matthew 5:19.) Read **Hebrews 9:27**. When will the judgment (court in Heaven) be held for non-believers? _____ _____ The word *judgment* in this verse is the same word as in Matthew 5:21 which talks about the fact that those who murder are in danger of the judgment. Hebrews 9:27 is referring to those who die without Christ as their Lord and Savior. So those who are not believers will stand before God *after their death* and be judged by their works at the Great White Throne Judgment. It will be proven they never had a changed life and were not ever saved from their sins. (See Revelation 20:11-15.) Matthew 25:32 says, "All the nations will be gathered before Him, and He will separate them one from another, as a shepherd divides his sheep from the goats." According to the terminology in this verse, God will separate those who are sheep (his children, Christians) from those who are goats (non-Christians). The only thing that matters in a court is the final decision from the judge, so the only thing that really matters is what God decides. We do not have to be afraid of the judgment of God at our death if we have been saved by faith in Jesus Christ.

We will learn more proofs of a real believer later in this Bible study. For now, let's see what God says is the way He allows someone to experience a new birth as a true Christian. To know this, we must learn what God is like and how He views you.

True Love

As a new mother, I wrapped my son in his soft blue blanket and huddled him close as I stepped out of my car into the bitter cold air on a January morning. Not seeing the logs stacked on the rock path below, I found myself falling with my baby! I had to think quickly to protect my precious son from serious injury, even death, so I intentionally twisted my body, turning it around in mid-air, choosing to tumble onto the rocky path, so my baby would be cushioned by falling on my body. When we hit the logs and rocks, I had made it half way around, but my knee and back hit the rough path hard. My baby, cushioned by my body, suffered only a slight scrape on his leg. I was in severe pain that lasted for months, but an immeasurable feeling of relief filled my heart because my baby was safe from harm. This true story reminds us of God's love for you and me. He loves you so much that He sacrificed Himself and chose to be hurt on purpose, dying in your place so you would not have to die for your sins. True love thinks of others more than self. That's what Jesus did for you. He loves you more than any mother loves her baby.

Realize God Loves You

Jeremiah 31:3b says, "I have loved you with an everlasting love." Write your name in this verse. "I have loved _____ with an everlasting love." He loves you because "God is love" (1 John 4:8b). God loves you more than you can comprehend! God loves the past, present, and future you. He knows everything about you and yet He still loves you. He loved you many years ago, and He loves you today. God will love you forever. God is not like a human being. Humans tend to love others conditionally—if a person makes us feel good, or treats us right, or meets our needs. But God loves you unconditionally. Read **Romans 8:35-39.** Tell in one word what will separate us from the love of Christ? _____

Read **Psalm 27:10.** Who will love you when others reject you? _____ Can anyone or anything keep God from loving you? _____ The *LORD* will always be faithful to love you. He will never reject you. *Nothing* will separate us from the love of Christ!

- **God is _____.** Read **Psalm 99:9b.**

Have you ever searched for love in a person only to be disappointed? People cannot love perfectly; only God can. He has never thought a wrong thought or performed a wrong deed; therefore, His love is not based on how we treat Him or what happens to us or what we look like. God is able to love you perfectly and unselfishly because He is holy. God is so *holy* (without sin), that He loves you perfectly.

- **God Cares about _____.** Read **Psalm 138:8.**

He cares about what you care about, and He will perfect your situation, bringing to pass His will concerning you. This does not mean you will receive everything you desire, but that you will receive what is best for your life, according to God's plan and right timing for you. God has great compassion for you and understands how your difficulties are hurting you each day. He will accomplish what is best in you as you continue to pray and obey His Word. But you must decide to trust God with your problems and future and not worry. If you fear or worry, you will not experience the joy God has for you in the midst of trials. When you are His child, He is actively involved in the details of your life. He experiences the joyous times with you as well as the hurtful, sad times you go through. He has the strength, wisdom, and power to love you perfectly and help you with any problem. He will never leave or forsake you because He has made you (Heb. 13:5). He is a personal God. You can say, "God cares about whatever concerns *me*!" (Did you fill in all the blanks?)

DAY 2
True Love's Source

Read memory verses, references, and Gospel points five times each.

<u>**Memory Verses and Gospel Points (GP):**</u>

1. **<u>GP1:</u>** God loves you! (John 3:16; Jeremiah 31:3)
   <u>**John 3:16**</u> "For God so loved the world that He gave His only begotten Son, that whoever believes in Him should not perish, but have everlasting life."

2. **<u>GP2</u>:** All have sinned. (Romans 3:23, 5:8, 6:23; Luke 13:3; Ephesians 2:8-9)
   <u>**Romans 3:23**</u> "For all have sinned and fall short of the glory of God."

3. **<u>Romans 5:8</u>** "But God demonstrates His own love toward us, in that while we were still sinners, Christ died for us."

Lord Jesus, please clean me of anything that would distract and hinder me from learning who You are today. Reveal more of Your awesome character and how great Your love is for me. In Jesus' name, Amen.

Billy Graham said, "God proved his love on the Cross. When Christ hung, and bled, and died, it was God saying to the world, 'I love you.'"[1] Are you glad God showed His love through the cross? _____ He also showed you His love way before the cross. Read below to find out. Look up the verses and find the answers to write in the blanks.

- **God is the _____.** Read **Genesis 1:1-2:3.**

Another reason He loves you is because He created you. He is the *Creator*. According to this passage, what did God create on each day? Fill in the blanks that are not filled in for you.

Day 1: <u>light</u>   Day 2: He divided the waters between earth and sky.
Day 3: _____
Day 4: <u>sun, moon, stars, and time</u>   Day 5: _____
Day 6: _____

God does everything just right. He created the heavens and the earth. At first, it was dark on the earth and there was only water everywhere. Then He created light just by His verbal command and it became the first day. On the second day, He spoke and divided the waters between the earth and the sky. On the third day, He told the *dry land to appear* on the earth and *gathered the* seas together. Then He said for the earth to bring forth *grass, herbs (plants) with seeds, and fruit trees with seeds in them*. Now the earth is almost ready for creatures and humans to be alive. On the fourth day, He declared the sun, moon, and stars, (including the planets) into existence for light on the earth, for signs, and started the process of time with seasons, days, and years. On the fifth day, God commanded the oceans, rivers, and lakes to be filled with *sea creatures* and all sorts of *fish*. He also added *birds* of all species to the sky. Now it was time to fill the land. On the sixth day, God spoke *all animals and creeping things* into existence. Then God saved the best for last. He made humans, a *man and a woman*. Next, God spoke and chose to make us in His own image. But He did not speak to create man and woman with life like He did the other creation. He took the time to form Adam, the first man, out of the dust of the ground and breathed into his nostrils the breath of life (Genesis 2:7) and He made Eve, the first woman, from the rib of Adam (Genesis 2:22.) He made us male and female so we could reproduce more people and glorify Him. How marvelous that God would make us in His likeness and take time to breathe life into mankind! God rested on the seventh day. What did God say about all of His creation? (See Genesis 1:31). _____ It was *very good*! Now that you know how you and the earth began, do you feel loved yet? Just think—God created a whole universe for you!

Since God created men and women to be like Him, we must be very special. Think about it. You were created by God, for God, in God's image and likeness, and for His glory (Genesis 1:26-27; Galatians 2:20; 1 Peter 4:11). God made you with a mind that has the ability to think intelligently and to see things in a spiritual sense; but you and other people are not equal with God. The Creator made mankind to worship Him. He is greater than all of the creation He brought into existence. Even though God made people and animals, He made us different. Human beings are higher than animals, and we are to rule over animals and all of creation responsibly (Genesis 1:28). No human being ever evolved from an animal. You came from Adam, and you are very different from an animal because you were specially created in God's image. This does not mean you are a god, but that you are a wonderful human creation started by our Creator.

How are we different from God? God has emotions, and so do people. But God does not make decisions based on His emotions, but on what is right (Romans 3:22-26; Revelation 19:11). God has all knowledge, wisdom, and understanding! (Psalm 104:24; Isaiah 40:28; Romans 11:33). We do not have all knowledge, but we are able to think, reason, and be creative because of the limited knowledge God has given us. God is a Spirit (John 4:24; Proverbs 15:3) and can be everywhere at one time, seeing everything. But people have flesh and are limited in mobility. God loves you in spite of your imperfections, and you are able to love others more and more as you become more like God in character through daily time spent with Him.

Amy Carmichael said, "Cruelty and wrong are not the greatest forces in the world. There is nothing eternal in them. Only love is eternal."[2] Human flesh is not eternal, but God is eternal and holy (without sin). That is why He can love you perfectly. Real love comes from God and will last forever (Jeremiah 31:3). He will never stop loving you. When did He start loving you? See below.

- **God Loved You Before You Were** _____. Read **Psalm 139:1-18.**

What are some ways God shows that He loves you in the above verses? _____
_____
_____
_____

How many ways did you find? _____ God loves you more than any other person is capable of loving you. God loves you even though He knows every good and bad thing about you. He is the perfect Father and delights in the unique person you are now. His love is not based on any of your accomplishments, but loves you regardless of achievements, or lack of them. He loved you so much that He took care of you when you were being formed inside your mother and kept a record of your parts as you were being made. You are a special creation, *born* with a special purpose and plan. God thinks about you all the time. He totally loves you. God has shown His love to you in many ways and still does so every day through protecting you, healing you physically, and taking care of you because He is the perfect Heavenly Father.

- **God is the** _____**of the Bible.** Read **2 Timothy 3:16.**

We know these things are true about God because God is the *author* of the Bible. His holiness guarantees the Bible to be true. God gave His inspiration to "secretaries" He used to write down what He wanted to say in the Word of God, the Holy Bible. They wrote what God, the Holy Spirit, told them to write, no more and no less. It was from God's thoughts, not their thoughts. That is why there are no errors in the ancient scrolls, the Holy Scriptures. 2 Peter 1:21 says, "For prophecy never came by the will of man, but holy men of God spoke as they were moved by the Holy Spirit."

- **God is** _____. Read **John 17:17**.

John 17:17 says, "Sanctify them by Your truth. Your word is truth." Because our holy God wrote the Bible, we can have confidence that it is totally accurate in its every page. The truth in His Word reveals to us how to live with Him in eternity, shows us how to have a personal relationship with Jesus on earth, and nurtures our friendship with our Heavenly Father. The Bible shows us what is right so we will be protected from what is wrong and explains correct beliefs in every area so we can discern error in any philosophy we may hear from other views. Reading and studying the Scriptures prepares us to make successful decisions in our daily life, and so much more. Everything we believe must be based on the *truth* of God's holy Word.

- **God is Preparing a** _____ **for You.** Read **John 14:2-3**.

God is preparing a beautiful *place* for you in heaven. Heaven is not a figment of your imagination. It is not just a bunch of clouds and singing. It is a real place with mansions (an abode or home, a residence, or place to stay) and a street of gold (Revelation 21:21). The foundations of the buildings are built out of many different, colorful, precious stones. The gates are made of pearl, and there is a river of life. There is also a tree of life that produces a different fruit each month. There are saints (those who have been saved) who live there. There are angels, too. Angels were not previously people. No place in Scripture does it say that believers (saints) turn into angels. We will be worshiping God, not angels (Revelation 22:8-9). There is plenty of light and no darkness whatsoever. Heaven is like earth in many ways, only much better. Read more about heaven in Chapter 21 of Revelation.

Now you know that God *created* you, *loved you before you were born,* is the *Author* of the Bible, the source of all *truth,* and He is preparing a *place* for you in heaven. You can rejoice no matter what happens today because you have a wonderful future ahead of you with your perfect Father! The true love offered to you is available only through God. Have a great day knowing you are loved by Jesus. (Remember to fill in the answers.)

An Enemy to Conquer

Try learning the memory verses and Gospel Points by playing a game. See Appendix B.

Memory Verses and Gospel Points (GP):

1. **GP1:** God loves you! (John 3:16 and Jeremiah 31:3)
   John 3:16 "For God so loved the world that He gave His only begotten Son, that whoever believes in Him should not perish but have everlasting life."

2. **GP2:** All have sinned. (Romans 3:23; 5:8; 6:23; Luke 13:3; Ephesians 2:8-9)
   Romans 3:23 "For all have sinned and fall short of the glory of God."

3. **Romans 5:8** "But God demonstrates His own love toward us, in that while we were still sinners, Christ died for us."

Father, please open my eyes to see the truths in Your Word today. Help me to learn about the real enemy in my life so I can have victory as You have planned for me. In Jesus' name, Amen.

Realize You Have an Enemy

There is a story of a lady who worked for a sales company. She moved up to a higher position and later discovered that her boss was doing some illegal things. She had not done anything wrong, but realized she would go down with the company if she did not turn them in when she had found out about it. So she planned to remove the evidence from her computer and turn it in to the police. The boss must have decided to cover up his illegal activity, so he arranged for all the computers in his office to be stolen, so it looked like they were robbed. This happened just before the police were coming to get the evidence. Her boss somehow found out about her plans, so he went after her to take away any possibilities of her ever working in that field of work again. As a result, she could not find work. He even arranged to take away her house, her credit, and even hired someone to try and murder her! Thankfully, she escaped. But she knew too much and could not ever rest knowing that an enemy was out to destroy her. Thankfully, she found someone to help her and got into a protection program, but her life was never the same again. What if you knew someone was trying to destroy your life, but you did not know who it was? You have an enemy that is much worse than what the lady in this story experienced! But there is a way to conquer this enemy. Let's find out how this is possible.

- **What is Sin?**

1. How is sin described in this verse? 1 John 3:4 says, "Whoever commits sin also commits lawlessness, and sin is lawlessness." _____

Because heaven is a perfect place, there is one thing that can never be in heaven, or else it would totally ruin heaven. That is sin (Revelation 21:27). Sin is an enemy of heaven, and it is the enemy in you. It contaminates your life. Just as you do not want to drink water out of a dirty glass, heaven cannot be contaminated with the dirtiness (*lawlessness*) of sin, or it would not be heaven. Sin is like being contaminated on the inside. It is breaking God's law. When we sin, we are breaking the law just like a criminal, and that makes us guilty before God. Sin can be defined as anything you think, do, or say that does not please God and breaks His laws.

2. According to that simple definition, write several examples of sins that people think, say, and do. Proverbs 23:7 says, "For as he thinks in his heart, so is he." (See Galatians 5:19-21 for a partial list of sins.)

a) Sins people <u>think</u>: _____
Job 2:10b – "In all this Job did not sin with his lips."
Psalm 39:1 – "I said, I will guard my ways, lest I sin with my tongue."

b) Write sins people <u>say</u>: _____
James 4:17—"Therefore, to him who knows to do good and does not do it, to him it is sin."
Read **Galatians 5:16-17**. There is a war between the _____ and our _____.

c) Sins people <u>do</u>: _____

d) Good deeds people <u>do not do.</u> This is sin also. (Ex: <u>Not being kind, not attending church regularly</u>) _____

- **Who has Sinned?**

1. People are not perfect. There is a war between the *Spirit* of God in us and our *flesh*. Originally, God desired for men and women to be created perfect and without a sin nature. But from the very beginning, God gave humans a choice to love and obey God or go their own way. Sadly, when mankind sinned in the Garden of Eden, our flesh inherited a desire to think, say, and do wrong. Now we are prone to sin apart from the divine influence from God (Romans 7:18). But we still have a choice. Read **James 2:10.** How is guilt determined? Is it by how many things we did right? Or is it by one sin we did, said, or thought? _____. The law is concerned only with the truth. Did the person commit the crime or not? This is what James 2:10 means. It does not matter how good we are, only that we have sinned against God. We are not perfect; therefore, we are guilty of sin. Are you guilty? _____

2. Only God is perfect. Jesus is God and that means He is perfect. "In Him there is no sin" (1 John 3:5b). Romans 3:23 says, "For all have sinned, and fall short of the glory of God." Are you a sinner? _____ Romans 5:8 and 10 says, "But God demonstrates His own love toward us, in that while we were still sinners, Christ died for us... For if when we were enemies we were reconciled to God through the death of His Son, much more, having been reconciled, we shall be saved by His life." When did God die for us? He died while we were what? _____ What relationship did we have with God before we were reconciled (changed from the inside)? _____ It is comforting to know that while you were still a *sinner*, God loved you enough to allow His Son Jesus to die for you so you could be saved and live with Him someday. God also loved you while you were still *His enemy*! Would you ever die for an enemy? _____ He loved you, not your sin. That is a lot of love!

- **Where did Sin Start?**

1. We were born with a sin nature. Read **Jeremiah 17:9**. According to this verse, evil comes from our _____. Wicked thoughts come from inside of who we are—our *hearts*. We desire to sin from deep within ourselves (Prov. 21:10a). Because we are born sinners, our thoughts will naturally be evil. We all know how to do wrong, having a sinful nature.

2. How did evil come into the world? Genesis Chapter 3 tells us about the first sin and its curse that passed down to every human being on earth. We know this because the Bible says in Romans 5:12, "Therefore, just as through one man sin entered the world, and death through sin, and thus death spread to all men, because all sinned." Read **Psalm 51:5**. Where did you get the iniquity curse according to this verse? _____ _____ You and I were born with a sin disease. We were *conceived in sin and sin was passed down to us*. It may not be our fault that we were born that way, but it is our fault if we choose to do wrong, and every person on earth is guilty. We must be cured of our sin disease, or we will die in our reprobate, wicked state. Jesus has the cure! But first, we must know that our wrong desires, thoughts, and deeds must be punished.

3. How can we be rescued from this punishment? Check all the ways a person can be saved (rescued from the penalty of sin) according to God's Holy Word.

____ Being more good than bad   ____ Going to church
____ Being baptized   ____ Keeping all 10 Commandments
____ Not being immoral   ____ Attending confirmation
____ Being religious, sincere in what I believe   ____ Giving money to charities
____ Being baptized as a baby   ____ Born into a religious family
____ Obeying all the teachings of the church
____ Believing in Jesus, the Only Son of God, Who gave His blood, died, rose again; confess Him as Lord with my mouth.

There is only one right answer according to God's Word. Find out if your answer was correct tomorrow.

DAY 4

The Conqueror's Plan

Read memory verses, references, and Gospel points five times each or play a memory game.

Memory Verses and Gospel Points (GP):

1. **GP1:** God loves you! (John 3:16 and Jeremiah 31:3)
   John 3:16 "For God so loved the world that He gave His only begotten Son, that whoever believes in Him should not perish but have everlasting life."

2. **GP2:** All have sinned. (Romans 3:23; 5:8; 6:23; Luke 13:3; Ephesians 2:8-9)
   Romans 3:23 "For all have sinned and fall short of the glory of God."

3. **Romans 5:8** "But God demonstrates His own love toward us, in that while we were still sinners, Christ died for us."

_____

God, Thank you for loving me even though I was Your enemy because of my sin. Cause me to be open to Your plan of victory so I can conquer the enemy of sin in my life. In Jesus' name, Amen.

He Took My Whipping

There is a story told of a boy whom we will call Tom. He lived in the days when there were one-room school houses. One morning, after he had walked to school, he was so hungry that he stole another boy's lunch. The schoolmaster found out about it and told Tom he would have to take a lashing because stealing was a sin. An older, stronger boy by the name of Joshua noticed how skinny, malnourished, and poor Tom was, and he felt sorry for him. He told the schoolmaster, "Sir, I'll take Tom's whipping." The schoolmaster was surprised, but agreed. Tom's mouth flew wide open. He could not believe that someone would take his beating for him. He felt a sense of relief. But Tom cried throughout the spanking as he watched his strong friend take his punishment in his place. It was awful as well as wonderful.[3] This reminds me of what Jesus did for you. He took your whipping for sin when He died in your place on the cross. Sin requires a payment. Either each one of us lets Jesus pay for our wickedness and be disciplined for it, or we take the punishment ourselves.

- **What is the Payment for Sin?**

1. Read **Romans 6:23** and find out the answer. "Wages" simply means "payment." Because God cannot break His own law (or else He would be sinning), He has to have a payment or punishment for it. According to Romans 6:23, what is the payment or punishment for sin? _____ A spiritual death means to be separated from God forever. It means that

anyone who has sinned has to die. So we are all condemned to be punished for our evil by *death*. Do not give up. There is good news coming!

John 3:17-18 says, "For God did not send his Son into the world to condemn the world, but that the world through him might be saved. He who believes in him is not condemned; but he who does not believe is condemned already, because he has not believed in the name of the only begotten Son of God."

2. Did God send Jesus into the world to condemn you? _____ Why did He come? __ _____ Are you glad God loved you enough to take the condemnation for your sin? _____ He wants *the world to be saved*, that is, rescued from the punishment for our sin. Have you ever noticed that a thief thinks he will never get caught, but he always makes one mistake that gets him caught? Why is that? It is because there is a principle (law) of sin. Numbers 32:23b says, "Be sure your sin will find you out." That means it will be found out. Evil cannot be hidden. God knows it all, so there is no escaping the payment/ punishment for sin other than the choices God gives us. It is simple. There are two choices to make sure your sin is paid for. Decide which is better.

a) **Choice one**: You can choose to pay for your sin with your own life by dying and being separated from God forever in a place of torment called hell. God prepared hell for the devil and his demons, not people, but humans will suffer in hell if they choose to ignore God's gift. (Matthew 25:41).

OR

b) **Choice two**: Allow Jesus, God's only Son, to shower the greatest love gift of all on you by providing Himself as a substitute and giving His blood to die and pay for your sin. What a sacrifice! What love He has for you!

Which way do you choose? Will you pay for your own sin or allow Jesus to pay for you? _____ _____

• **Is There another Way to Pay for Sin's Punishment?**

Can a person be saved from the penalty of sins by doing good works? _____ Notice what God's Word says about it:

Titus 3:5 says, "Not by works of righteousness which we have done, but according to his mercy he saved us, through the washing of regeneration and renewing of the Holy Spirit."

Ephesians 2:8-9 says, "For by grace you have been saved through faith, and that not of yourselves; it is the gift of God, not of works, lest anyone should boast."

1. What do Titus 3:5 and Ephesians 2:8-9 say about how to be saved from being punished for sin? _____ _____

2. Does God require "good works" in order for you to become a saved child of God? _____
    (Fill in the blanks by referring to the verses listed above.)

    Titus 3:5a – "_____ by _____ of righteousness which we have done, but according to His _____ He saved us."

    Eph. 2:8 and 9a - "For by _____ you have been saved through _____, and that _____ of _____; it is the _____ of God, _____ of _____, lest anyone should _____."

> "No matter who we are or what we have done, we are saved only because of what Christ has done for us. I will not go to Heaven because I have preached to great crowds. I will go to Heaven for one reason: Jesus Christ died for me, and I am trusting Him alone for my salvation."
> – Billy Graham

The verses are very clear. The obvious answer is no. God does not require any works for us to be saved. There is no other way to pay for sin's punishment except through the death and resurrection of Jesus Christ. Billy Graham said, "No matter who we are or what we have done, we are saved only because of what Christ has done for us. I will not go to Heaven because I have preached to great crowds. I will go to Heaven for one reason: Jesus Christ died for me, and I am trusting Him alone for my salvation."[4] If Billy Graham cannot go to heaven because of all the good he has done, do you think we will? Not one person can ever be good enough to take away the punishment for his or her sin.

Every other religion in the world does <u>not</u> teach the whole truth. They make up requirements of good works, a list that people have to do and not do in order to be forgiven, go to heaven, or please their god. Other religions are false because they say you are your own "savior" by doing good deeds.

Christianity is different because it is <u>the truth from God</u>, and it says that Jesus is the Savior who paid it all. It is a free gift given by grace, only waiting for the person to accept it. God's love will overcome the enemy if you will only let Him. Yesterday, you were asked to check all the ways to be saved. The only correct answer according to God's Word was: "Believing in Jesus, the Only Son of God who gave His blood, died, rose again and confessing Jesus as Lord with my mouth." Let's find out how this is possible tomorrow. (Did you check to see if all your blanks are filled in today?)

DAY 5
My Commander's Qualifications

Read memory verses, references, and Gospel points five times each.

Memory Verses and Gospel Points (GP):

1. **GP1:** God loves you! (John 3:16 and Jeremiah 31:3)
   John 3:16 "For God so loved the world that He gave His only begotten Son, that whoever believes in Him should not perish but have everlasting life."

2. **GP2**: All have sinned. (Romans 3:23; 5:8; 6:23; Luke 13:3; Ephesians 2:8-9)
   Romans 3:23 "For all have sinned and fall short of the glory of God."

3. **Romans 5:8** "But God demonstrates His own love toward us, in that while we were still sinners, Christ died for us."

Lord Jesus, You are the only One qualified to conquer my war with sin. Reveal more of who You are and do not allow anything to distract my mind from Your truths. In Jesus' name, Amen.

Did you know that God is your Commander? There is an ongoing war between righteousness and evil. He commands His angels to fight for you every day because He loves you. What is your Commander like? You already know that He loves you, even though you started out as His enemy because of your sin. But now He has provided a marvelous plan so you do not have to be punished for your wrong deeds. What a love story!

The Mother Hen
There is a story told by some firemen who fought in a forest fire. After the fire was put out, the firemen were walking through the area to make sure all flames were really out, when one fireman came across a dead hen. He was surprised to see it because the hen could have flown away to get out of a forest fire. When he turned the burnt mother hen over, he was amazed to see little chicks alive under her wings! It was obvious what had happened. That mother hen, who could have escaped the fire, stayed and gave up her life to cover her chicks with her wings to protect them from the fire. She gave her life so her children could live. This story reminds us of what Jesus did for us all. He came to earth and went through the fire of persecution, and then to the cross to die in our place, so we could live forever with Him!

Believe Who Jesus Christ Is:

- Read **John 1:1-5. God has always** _____.

Let's start at the beginning. The beginning is <u>before</u> Jesus came as a Baby in the flesh. He was alive as God's Son in heaven before He came to earth. God has always *existed*. Who is the "Word"?

_____

God wrote the Word of God, the Bible, but the "Word" in this passage means this is another one of His names that tells us who He is. The Word is *God's Son, Jesus Christ*.

- Read **John 3:16. Jesus is the** _____ _____ **of God.**

Jesus is the *only Son* of God, holy (perfect) just like God the Father. He did not have other brothers or sisters that were God. He had half brothers and sisters (in the flesh) on earth born as Mary and Joseph's children. But there is no other God, except for God the Father, Jesus the Son, and the Holy Spirit. God is three persons, but <u>one</u> God. (We will learn more about this aspect of God later in this study.)

- Read **Matthew 1:18-25. God the Son came to Earth in the** _____.

Jesus willingly came to earth and agreed to take on human flesh so He could ultimately die for the sins of mankind. He was on earth for thirty-three years in a human body. He came to earth, clothed in *flesh*, as a baby.

Joseph and Mary were engaged to be married. But when Joseph heard from Mary that she was pregnant, he thought Mary had been unfaithful to him because he knew that he had nothing to do with the pregnancy. He loved her still, but what did he decide to do in verse 19? _____
_____ When Joseph and Mary lived, during this culture and time period, it was the accepted practice to stone a woman who was pregnant out of wedlock, but Joseph decided to *put her away privately* instead. Read what happened next.

- Read **Matthew 1:18, 20-23. Jesus Christ was Born from Mary who was a** _____.

1. When did Mary become pregnant? Was it <u>before</u> she and Joseph had sex or <u>after</u> they were married and had sex? See verse 18. _____ This is very important in the Christian faith and shows that Mary was a *virgin* who was pregnant *before* she and Joseph came together. That may be impossible physically, but all things are possible with God. The fact that Mary was a virgin is confirmed in these verses. Name two reasons why the angel told Joseph not to be afraid to take Mary as his wife: _____

_____

_____

The angel verified that *Mary was pregnant with child of the Holy Spirit* and Joseph believed the angel. Also, another proof that Mary was a virgin is the fact that it was predicted that Jesus (who was inside her) would *save His people from their sins.* An accidental pregnancy in sin (outside of marriage) would never produce God, the Holy Savior! (By the way, God was never born. He has always been all God. There came a time when He put on human flesh and became all Man also. But God has always existed and will always be eternal.) This birth was planned by God and He put Jesus, the Messiah, inside Mary.

2. Read **Luke 2:8-20**. In verses 13-14, what happened when Jesus was born? _____
_____
_____

It was also verified that Mary was a virgin and pregnant with child of the Holy Spirit when a *group of shepherds was visited by a host of angels who sang praises to God to announce the birth of our Savior, Jesus, and to proclaim peace and goodwill to mankind.* The shepherds were so excited that they told everyone they saw (verses 17-18). Would shepherds (or anyone) agree on what they saw if it were not true? You know how people are when they are witnesses to an accident or any event; one person hears and sees it one way, and the next person sees it another way. That is another miracle, the fact that they all told the same story. Then of course, the miracles in the life of Jesus later also proved it was true that He was the Son of God.

•   Read **Isaiah 9:6. Jesus is All** _____.

Jesus came down from heaven. He is God, just like His Father and the Holy Spirit. The whole Bible confirms that Jesus is totally God. Many changed lives prove that Jesus was and is who He said He is. We have seen how Jesus came in the flesh. That meant He was and is all Man: He was completely and fully human, except without sin. Now let's look at the fact that *Jesus is all God* too. "All God" means He is completely and fully God. He is not part Man and part God.

What are five names that are connected to the Child that is born and the Son that is given in this verse? _____
_____
_____

The Child and Son are the same Jesus, who is truly the Mighty God and equal with the Father God and Holy Spirit in power, authority, and position. They are one God, expressed in three roles or persons (1 John 5:7). Now you know your Commander's qualifications just as the title describes!

Following are the answers to the bullet points in this devotion. From John 1:1-5, God the Father, Son, and Holy Spirit have always *existed.* From John 3:16, they chose one day in time to send Jesus, the *Only Son* of God, down to earth to be born in human (Matthew 1:18-25) *flesh* which means He is a real human Man. From Matthew 1:18,20-23, Jesus was born of Mary who was a *virgin,* not from a human father, and was perfectly holy and without sin. From Isaiah 9:6, He is also *all God.* His names in this verse are *"Wonderful," "Counselor," "Mighty God," "Everlasting Father," "Prince of Peace."* Our Commander is all God and all Man in one. He is the only One qualified to conquer the enemy of sin. Let's continue to look at how this is possible tomorrow.

DAY 6

True Love Conquers the Enemy

Play the erase game or another memory game with the verses and Gospel points below.

Memory Verses and Gospel Points (GP):

1. **GP1:** God loves you! (John 3:16 and Jeremiah 31:3)
    John 3:16 "For God so loved the world that He gave His only begotten Son, that whoever believes in Him should not perish but have everlasting life."

2. **GP2:** All have sinned. (Romans 3:23; 5:8; 6:23; Luke 13:3; Ephesians 2:8-9)
    Romans 3:23 "For all have sinned and fall short of the glory of God."

3. **Romans 5:8** "But God demonstrates His own love toward us, in that while we were still sinners, Christ died for us."

Father God, allow my eyes to be opened to the magnitude of what You sacrificed for me so I could be saved from the punishment of my sin forever! In Jesus' name, Amen.

Could there have been another way to rescue mankind? Read below and find out.

The Bird Man

There was a man who wanted to help some birds who kept flying into his house. The birds were being killed by flying into his windows, but no matter what he did to assist them, the birds were more afraid of him every time he tried to rescue them. He told a friend, "If only I could become a bird, then I could communicate to them that I care and I am trying to help them. Then they would not be afraid of me, and I could save their lives." His friend replied to this man who did not yet believe in Jesus, "That is why Jesus became a man, so He could reveal His love to you in a way you could understand. Then you could know that He loves you and could save your life forever if you believe in Him." The man finally understood. The best way to rescue the birds was to become a bird. The best way to rescue mankind was to become a man.[5] Jesus did for me what I could not do for myself. There was no other way. Now that we know who Jesus is, what did Jesus do for you that is so important?

Believe What Jesus Christ Did

* **Jesus is the Only** _____.

Read **John 14:6.** Is there any other way to get to God the Father? _____ How do we get to God the Father? _____ The only way to get to God the Father is through *Jesus.* John 10:10b says, "I am come that they may have life and have it more abundantly." John 10:9 says, "I am the door. If anyone enters by Me, he will be saved, and will go in and out and find pasture." There is only one door, one *way,* and it is Jesus Christ. Jesus Christ is our mediator. (Read **1 Timothy 2:5**).

Have you ever known the son of the president or king of a country? You cannot just walk right up to a president or king of any country unless you are on staff or have a high position of authority. But if you are friends with the child of a president or king, then that child can get you the permission to enter. Jesus is not only your mediator; He is your friend (John 15:13-14), and you can be adopted as His child (John 1:12), so when you know Jesus, you know the Father God. If we say that Jesus is the only way to be saved from our sins, then some people may say that we are narrow minded. Jesus would agree (Matthew 7:13-14). But the truth is that Jesus is the only way; our only door to God.

Rescued from Death

Have you ever been in a position to rescue a friend from death? A man rescued me from drowning in a very rough river a long time ago. We were whitewater rafting, and our boat became caught in a strong current, so we were stuck. The weight of the passengers and the current together started pulling us down until I was even with the water. I was about to go under the churning, rough water with no way to pull myself back up. But thankfully, just in time, a man's hand reached down and pulled me up. I was so thankful to him for saving my life! I was totally at his mercy. There was no other way for me to be saved. I could have argued with this man that I did not want to be rescued that way. I could have said, "This is too embarrassing; I will get out of this predicament myself another way." But that would have been foolish. Thank God He provided the way to saving my life. There is only one way to save your life from the punishment for sin and only one way to the One and only true God.

* **Jesus Died for You when You were His** _____.

1. What are four conditions Jesus found you in when he decided to die for you? God has shown love to you when you were His *enemy.* Read **Romans 5:6-10.** (See vs. 6, 8, and 10.)
   a) _____ b) _____
   c) _____ d) _____

Every human being on earth was in the position of being *without strength, ungodly, still a sinner* and *God's enemy* because of sin. But He still loves you and all people.

2. What six ways did God show His forgiveness to you? (See verses 8, 9, and 10.)
   a)_____ b) _____
   c) _____ d) _____
   e) _____ f) _____

(a) God *showed His own love even though you were still a sinner (b) by dying for you. (c)* He *justified you* by *giving His blood* on the cross. "Justified" means "just as if I have never done wrong." *(d)* Jesus *saved you from the wrath of God on sin* through Himself. Wrath is God's anger against iniquity which is punishment in hell, but He loves you. *(e)* He brought you to God *(reconciled, changed you)* by making you in right standing with Him, *through the death of His Son. (f) He saved you by giving His life as a substitute* in your place. We became His enemies because of the sin disease in us from birth. But we choose to be God's enemies each day when we disobey Him. Jesus, God the Son, died for you so you could now become His friend forever, His child, and live with Him in His eternal home.

- Jesus _____ Took Your _____.

Was Jesus forced to go to the cross or did He willingly take your punishment? Read **John 10:15b, 17b, and 18a** to find out and fill in each blank.

- Jesus _____ His Blood and _____.

What two important things happened on the cross that have everything to do with forgiving you and cleansing you of your sin? Read **1 John 1:7b; Hebrews 9:22b, and 1 Corinthians 15:3b.** (Hold your finger here.)

- Jesus was _____.

What important fact happened immediately after Jesus died to prove He was dead? Read **1 Corinthians 15:4a.** (Hint: It can be said in one word. Hold your finger in this verse for the next blank.)

- Jesus _____ again. He came back _____!

What else happened that is an essential foundation for the Christian faith? (See **1 Corinthians 15:4** again.)

- Jesus went back up to _____.

Where did Jesus go after seeing His disciples for about forty days? Read **Acts 1:9-11.**

Now you know who Christ is and what He did for you. He *willingly* took your *punishment* for sin. He *gave* His perfect blood and *died* for your sins. He was *buried*, proving He was dead and *rose* again, coming back *alive*! He went back up to *heaven* after forty days on earth following His resurrection. Tomorrow, find out how to conquer the enemy within you through God's sacrificial love for you.

Let's review. What are the main truths you learned in this chapter?

I. Realize God Loves You

A. God is Holy.
B. God Cares about Me.
C. God is the Creator.
D. God Loved You Before You Were Born.
E. God is the Author of the Bible.
F. God is Truth.
G. God is Preparing a Place for You.

II. Realize You Have an Enemy

A. What is Sin? Sin is breaking God's law by what we think, say, or do.
B. Who has Sinned? All people have sinned.
C. Where did Sin Start? After Adam, all humans were born with a sin nature.
D. What is the Payment for Sin? It is only through death.
E. Is There another Way to Pay for Sin's Punishment? No

III. Believe Who Jesus Christ Is

A. God has always Existed.
B. Jesus is the Only Son of God.
C. God the Son came to Earth in the Flesh.
D. Jesus Christ was Born from Mary who was a Virgin.
E. Jesus is All God.

IV. Believe What Jesus Christ Did

A. Jesus is the Only Way.
B. Jesus Died for You when You were His Enemy.
C. Jesus Willingly took Your Punishment.
D. Jesus Gave His Blood and Died.
E. Jesus was Buried.
F. Jesus Rose again. He came back Alive!
G. Jesus went back up to Heaven.

Are you glad God loves you even though sin made you His enemy? _____

Thank you, Jesus, for showing Your great love for me by conquering my sin and paying for it with Your life! In Jesus' name, Amen.

CHAPTER 2
The Evidences of God's Gift

DAY 1
The Greatest Gift

Read memory verses, references, and Gospel points five times each.

Memory Verses, Gospel Points, and Spiritual Gifts Profile:

1. **GP3**: Jesus, God's only Son, willingly paid for the punishment of your sin through His death, blood, burial, and coming back alive. (1 Corinthians 15:3-4; Hebrews 9:22b; 1 John 1:7b)
   1 John 1:7b "the blood of Jesus Christ His Son cleanses us from all sin."

2. **GP4**: What would you like for Jesus to do about your sin problem now?
   Romans 10:9 and 13 - "That if you confess with your mouth the Lord Jesus and believe in your heart that God has raised Him from the dead, you will be saved." "For whoever calls on the name of the LORD shall be saved."

3. Complete your **Spiritual Gifts Profile.** Turn in at the next meeting. (See Appendix H.)

Father, may You be honored and glorified today as I study the truths in the Bible. Help me to understand more deeply what the greatest gift is for me and all of mankind. May I find out today if I am just religious or truly believe in Jesus, the Son of God. In Jesus' name, Amen.

The Greatest Gift

What is the greatest gift you ever received? _____ When our son's birthday was approaching, we were looking forward to finding a special gift for him. He wanted a green machine for his birthday. It was like a big wheel bike for older kids. That is all he talked about. So we figured out how to sacrifice and save until we could surprise him with that unique present. We even made up a treasure hunt game so he could discover it. We had just as much fun giving the gift as it was for him to receive it. As his parents, we sacrificed to pay for the gift that we gave to our son. But it did not actually become his gift until he accepted it. This reminds me of what Jesus did for you and me. He sacrificed his life in order to pay for the best gift of all—forgiveness of all your sins, eternal life in heaven someday, becoming a child of God, and much more! But even though it is intended for you, it does not become your gift until you ACCEPT it. Let's find out how to accept such an expensive gift.

- **Has God's Love Conquered the Enemy of Sin in Your Life Yet?**

Is it enough to <u>know about</u> Jesus who wants to rescue you from sin? _____ Or do you need to come to know Him <u>personally</u> by accepting His free gift of eternal life? _____

1. Do you work for a gift? _____ Romans 6:23 says, "For the wages of sin is death, but the gift of God is eternal life through Christ Jesus our Lord." Who is giving the gift? _____ Who worked to give you the gift of eternal life? _____ The person who gave the gift works for the gift, right? _____ Have you ever worked for a gift? _____ If you worked for it, it was not a gift.

The Makeover

Some people think they have to clean up their lives by agreeing not to have fun anymore in order to become a Christian. But that is backwards thinking and not true. If you were to receive a gift that paid for you to get a makeover, would you be the one doing the makeover? _____ It would be the people who were paid to fix your hair and clothes and any other area that needed an overhaul. It reminds me of what Jesus does for you and me when we accept His free gift. We do not do the changing. Christ Jesus does the changing in us. We simply accept God's gift.

> "Am I born again or just religious?" Religion is what you do; Christianity is what Christ has done!

When we do that, a miracle happens, and we are cleansed of sin without doing anything ourselves. If we had to make ourselves become good and clean before God, that would be religion. Then why would we need God to do it? Ask yourself, "Am I born again or just religious?" Religion is what you do; Christianity is what Christ has done! Would Jesus have wasted thirty-three years away from His Father and gone through extreme pain to die for your sins if you could get rid of them yourself? _____ How do you accept such an awesome gift that changes you from the inside out—a makeover on the inside? Read on and see.

2. Who did Jesus come to help: good people or sinners? _____ "Jesus answered and said to them, Those who are well have no need of a physician; but those who are sick. I have not come to call the righteous, but sinners, to repentance" (Luke 5:31-32). In order to accept God's expensive but free gift, you must be willing to admit you need Jesus to take away your sins. Luke 13:3 says, "I tell you, no; but, unless you repent you will all likewise perish." Repentance is turning around and going the opposite direction. It is saying, "I am going the wrong way. I am turning around and going the right way now." It is following the right road toward God, instead of the wrong road toward sin.

The Unsaved Sunday School Teacher

A friend attended a seminar on *How to Lead People to Christ*, and she called the seminar leader the night it was over. She told her that she had been a Sunday School teacher for many years and had always believed in God. She thought she was a Christian. But that day she realized she had never repented by asking Jesus, her Lord, to forgive her of her sins. She did that when she got home that day. She admitted she was wrong and asked God to forgive and cleanse her of all evil. With God's help, she decided to turn to God, going in a new direction away from a life of serving her own flesh and toward obedience in Jesus as her Lord, her Boss, and Guide in life. Instantly, she had peace and was joyful and confident knowing God had truly saved her. There was a real heart change and she became a new creature in Christ!

The devil's fallen angels, called demons, believe in God and tremble in fear of Him (James 2:19), but they are not forgiven of their sins, nor will they submit to Jesus as Lord. If the demons who believe in God are not saved, then we must do more than believe God is real. We must be willing to turn away from our wrong ways and toward God. If anyone is too proud to admit he or she is a sinner and turn from sin, then that person will perish in hell. Jesus loves you so much that He did everything He could possibly do to make sure you do not have to pay for the punishment of your own evil doings. But there is one thing He cannot do. He cannot accept the gift for you. You are the only one who can repent and accept it. Continue reading to find out how to accept God's gift.

- **Who Must You Believe on to be Saved?** _____

God's Word says, "Believe on the Lord Jesus Christ, and you will be saved" (Acts 16:31b). Ephesians 4:6 says, "One God and Father of all, who is above all, and through all, and in you all." We cannot believe in two or more ways to be saved (rescued) from the punishment of our iniquities. Some people say they believe in Jesus and other gods or Jesus and good works. But no one can be rescued from sin any other way. What does God say in His Word? It says in Acts 4:10b, "By the name of Jesus Christ of Nazareth, whom you crucified, whom God raised from the dead, by Him this man stands here before you whole." Acts 4:12 says, "Nor is there salvation in any other, for there is no other name under heaven given among men by which we must be saved." There can be no other gods added. There can be no other good works added. We know that the name of *Jesus* is the only name that saves us from our sin. We all can have hope because Jesus has the answer! Continue finding out what it means to accept God's greatest gift tomorrow.

Accepting God's Gift

Read the memory verses and Gospel points five times each before starting your devotions.

Memory Verses, Gospel Points, and Spiritual Gifts Profile:

1. **GP3**: Jesus, God's only Son, willingly paid for the punishment of your sin through His death, blood, burial, and coming back alive. (1 Corinthians 15:3-4; Hebrews 9:22b; 1 John 1:7b)
1 John 1:7b "the blood of Jesus Christ His Son cleanses us from all sin."

2. **GP4**: What would you like for Jesus to do about your sin problem now?
Romans 10:9 and 13 - "That if you confess with your mouth the Lord Jesus and believe in your heart that God has raised Him from the dead, you will be saved." "For whoever calls on the name of the LORD shall be saved."

3. Complete your **Spiritual Gifts Profile.** Turn in at the next meeting.

Lord, may I accept Your free gift today or communicate more clearly to others how to receive it. In Jesus' name, Amen.

Accepting God's Gift

The Right Team

In the movie *The Blind Side*, a young man was offered a position on a football team with three different universities with a fully paid college education. What a huge gift! Each college enticed him with different bait by offering him the best of everything with extra bonus gifts too. He could not go with all three teams; he could choose only one. He finally decided on where he knew he would get the best education and could support that school from his heart. In a similar way, no one can choose all religions as the right way. You can be on only one team. Have you chosen to be on the team of the Lord Jesus Christ? _____ Jesus is the only way, the truth, and the life. There is only one right path to heaven. It is impossible to go two different directions at the same time. To accept God's free gift of salvation, each person must embrace His truth, therefore canceling out all others.

> You are not saved by good works, or good feelings, or any religion. There is only one true God, and He is **JESUS CHRIST.**

- **Jesus is the Only Way (Read John 14:6.)**

1. <u>Turn Away from the Wrong Ways</u>: Accepting Jesus as Savior and Lord means that you deny beliefs of all other religions. You are agreeing with God that you are not saved by good works, or good feelings, or any religion, and that you reject the belief that any god is the true God, other than JESUS CHRIST.

2. <u>Turn to the Right Way</u>: To accept God's gift of eternal life means you believe JESUS CHRIST is the ONLY WAY to be saved and repent of your sin according to the Bible. No one can add Jesus to his or her list of gods (Exodus 20:3) or add Christianity to the lists of beliefs and still be a true Christian. Jesus is the ONLY TRUE GOD. He has to be the ONLY LORD and first place in your life.

3. <u>Are you willing to accept Jesus as your Savior and surrender to Him as your Lord, the only true God, and make Him first place in your life</u>? _____ If so, tell Jesus what is in your heart, in your own words, using the A B C's below as your guide. What must I believe in order to be saved? _____
_____
_____

- **The Salvation ABC's**

The Bible says, "That if you <u>confess</u> with your mouth the <u>Lord</u> Jesus and <u>believe</u> in your heart that God has raised Him from the dead, you will be saved." "For whoever <u>calls</u> on the name of the LORD shall be saved" (Romans 10:9 and 13**)**. Also read **Luke 1:77 and 13:3** in your Bible. It tells us how anyone must repent of sin to be saved from the punishment of sin. It is not by any good works, but to:

1. **<u>ADMIT</u> to the Lord Jesus,** the Son of God who saves you and is in charge, whom you want to obey, that **you have sinned** (are wrong) and need Him to forgive you. And ask Him to be first in your life as your Lord too. (Psalm 51 is an example of repentance.)

2. **<u>BELIEVE</u> that Jesus gave His blood, died, was buried, and came back alive for your sins**. When you were born on this earth, there was a time and day you call your birthday. Jesus said, "You must be born again" (John 3:7b). If you want to be saved and be born again as God's child, there is a time and day you must choose to believe (know that it is true) that *Jesus died for your sins, gave His blood as payment for them, was buried, and came back alive.* You must believe He paid for your wrong deeds with the price of His blood and that He came back alive, not that it is just a historical fact. The difference in believing a historical fact and believing it in your heart is that you <u>act</u> on that belief. You must act on that belief, not by any good works, but by simply accepting God's gift with your mouth by faith and surrendering your will to Jesus as your Lord and Savior. Romans 10:10 says, "For with the heart one believes unto righteousness, and with the mouth confession is made unto salvation."

3. <u>**CALL**</u> **on the LORD Jesus' name, asking forgiveness for your sins and believing He gave His blood, died, was buried, and came back alive for you.** P.S. THIS IS HOW TO ACCEPT THE GIFT. You must accept this gift by telling God the (a) and (b) explanation of these verses: Romans 10:9 and 13. This is done with your mouth, not just your heart. It is calling on Jesus' name, confessing you are wrong, and repenting of your sin. "Repent" means to turn from sin to Jesus as your Lord. You also must believe He rose from the dead. Agreeing "Jesus is Lord" means you want Him to be in charge of your life. He is the only One you worship from now on. **Do you remember a time you ever told Jesus with your mouth that you repented of your sin and wanted to accept His gift of eternal life?** _____ Was it a genuine heart-felt desire? _____ Did you know the Holy Spirit was speaking to your heart that you needed to be saved?_____ Did Jesus become your **Savior** <u>and</u> **Lord**? _____ Did your life change from the inside and out? _____ You cannot go on what someone else told you or that another person prayed for you. <u>You</u> must be the one <u>who prayed and remembers the change</u>. If so, when was it? Write the date or if you do not know the date, write what you remember about it, making a picture in your memory. _____

_____

If you have not done this before, why not do it right now? It is not the words you say, but the attitude of a repentant, surrendered heart that desires Jesus as Savior and Lord that God hears from you. You can say a prayer similar to the one below. It is better if you tell God in your own words that you want Him to be your Lord and Savior. Below is only a guide.

Dear Heavenly Father,

<u>**Admit**</u> **to God you have sinned and repent of it.**
I am sorry that I have done, said, and thought wrong things. I need Your forgiveness. I repent (turn away from my sin). Please cleanse me. I turn to You to be my Father and ruler over all my life as my Lord, so I can start obeying You now with God's strength.

<u>**Believe**</u> **Jesus gave His blood, died, was buried, and came back alive for your sin.**
Father, I believe the Lord Jesus Christ is Your Son and He is God. Thank You, Jesus, for taking the punishment for my sin on the cross by dying in my place. I am grateful You paid for all the wrong things in me by cleaning me with Your holy blood and coming back alive.

<u>**Call**</u> **on Jesus' name after you have told Him (A) and (B) steps.**
Please save me and make me Your child. In <u>Jesus'</u> name, Amen.

- **Recording My New Birthday**

1. My Spiritual Birth Certificate

Did you talk to Jesus out loud in your own words or use the words under the ABC's as your guide? _____ Or were you already saved? _____
If you repented, made Jesus your Lord, and believed Jesus came back alive (praying in <u>Jesus' name</u>), then according to Romans 10:9-13 and John 1:12, you are in God's family now! If you did this just now or at an earlier date, then write down the date and place you received Jesus as your Savior and Lord in the Spiritual Birth Certificate below:

My Spiritual Birth Certificate

Heavenly Father: God

My Name: _____

Day/Month/Year: _____

Place: _____

Spiritual Birth Parent: _____
(Person who led you to Jesus)

Whether you just now accepted Jesus' gift or did it earlier in your life, you made the most important life-changing decision you could ever make! The enemy of sin has been conquered. Your sin disease is cured. If your salvation was real, you will have a changed life!

2. Record the Date in My Bible

If you did this, go write this record in your Bible now so you can remember that the date recorded in your spiritual birth certificate is your Christian birthday in God's family. You have two birthdays now (John 3:3-7). You have been born again! God has also recorded your heavenly birthday up in heaven. He has your name written down in the Book of Life, and it will never be erased (Luke 10:20; Revelation 3:5).

If you did not pray to accept God's gift today, do you remember a time that you told Jesus you wanted to be forgiven and believed in Him? _____ You can never be sure you are a saved, forgiven child of God if you do not remember actually asking Him for that yourself. Do not go on what someone may have told you that you did. Be sure <u>you</u> remember praying to be born into God's family. God remembers every time, but for your sake, to have a sure foundation to go back to, it is important that <u>you remember</u> a time, a picture in your mind, so you will be able to grow stronger in your faith in Jesus. John 3:11b says, "We speak what we know and testify what we have seen." If you do not know, make sure today.

Just as John 3:11 says, when you know you are saved, you will be able to write down your testimony of when you accepted Jesus Christ and surrendered to Him completely in your life. If you <u>said a prayer like the one given earlier</u> as an example AND have had a <u>changed life</u>, then write it down as a record for your own testimony on the next page.

3.   Write Down My Testimony

****

My Testimony

I was _____ years old.

I prayed for forgiveness of all my sins, acknowledging my belief in the resurrection of Jesus on ____
_____ (approximate) date.

Describe the scene: (example: at home in the blue chair, or at church, in a field on a sunny day, etc.) _____
_____
_____

My life changed in these ways after praying to repent of my sins and ask the Lord Jesus into my life: _____
_____
_____

Who did you tell first that you became a saved child of God (the church, a friend, a family member, a teacher)? Be specific. _____

****

4.   Tell Someone My Good News

It is important to tell someone who is a Christian what just happened to you. You can tell another friend in this Bible study or tell the whole church. They all will be so excited for you! You can even tell someone who is not a believer. It would be good for a lost person to hear about your conversion, although he or she will probably not be as excited since that person has not experienced salvation yet and may not understand. The Bible says in Matthew 10:32-33, "Therefore whoever confesses

Me before men, him I will also confess before My Father who is in heaven. But whoever denies Me before men, him I will also deny before My Father who is in heaven." In other words, if you are not ashamed of God, He will not be ashamed of you. According to this verse, if you tell someone that you are a child of God, then you are confessing Jesus before others. He will also tell others (in front of God the Father) that you are His son or daughter. But if you do not tell someone you are saved and continue to deny knowing Jesus and continue doing so until you die, then you are showing you are not really God's new creature. God will not allow His descendants to lose their salvation. A true believer will want to tell others that Jesus is his or her Father now, even if he or she is a little afraid. Psalm 118:6 says, "The Lord is on my side; I will not fear. What can man do to me?"

Remember to stop and <u>thank God right now</u> for saving you to be in His family. He will protect you now and will always be with you. Learn tomorrow how to know for sure that you will always be God's child and how to grow strong as a Christian.

DAY 3
God's Guarantee and My Evidence

Study memory verses and Gospel points. Say them five times each, or play the erase game.

Memory Verses, Gospel Points, and Spiritual Gifts Profile:

1. **GP3**: Jesus, God's only Son, willingly paid for the punishment of your sin through His death, blood, burial, and coming back alive. (1 Corinthians 15:3-4; Hebrews 9:22b; 1 John 1:7b)
   1 John 1:7b "The blood of Jesus Christ His Son cleanses us from all sin."

2. **GP4**: What would you like for Jesus to do about your sin problem now?
   Romans 10:9 and 13: "That if you confess with your mouth the Lord Jesus and believe in your heart that God has raised Him from the dead, you will be saved." "For whoever calls on the name of the LORD shall be saved."

3. Complete your **Spiritual Gifts Profile.** Turn in at the next meeting.

Lord, thank You that Your foundation is secure. Help every part of me to grasp the truths of Your faithful promises today as I study Your Word. May I understand more fully what it means to have the guarantee of eternal life and bask in this joy! In Jesus' name, Amen.

God's Guarantee

Do you know for sure that you were born on this earth? _____ How do you know? _____ _____Do you know because of the evidences you experience that show you are alive? There is also a legal birth certificate that has recorded your birth to guarantee you were born. God also has a record, a guarantee, to show that you have been born into His family.

- **God's Birth Certificate**

Read the record of your birth into God's family. 1 John 5:11-13 says, "And this is the record, that God hath given to us eternal life, and this life is in his Son. He that hath the Son hath life; and he that hath not the Son of God hath not life. These things have I written unto you that believe on the name of the Son of God; that ye may know that ye have eternal life, and that ye may believe on the name of the Son of God" (KJV). Yes, you can KNOW you are saved eternally when you believe in Jesus! You are saved by faith and by God's grace when you believe in Jesus' death on the cross, His burial, and that God raised Him from the dead and when you confessed your sins to Jesus as your Lord. Your spirit will KNOW that you have eternal life. There is a record, a testimony. He also has written your name in the Lamb's Book of Life in heaven as a record that you may enter heaven, your eternal home.

According to **Revelation 21:22-27**, can any sin enter heaven? _____ Who can enter heaven? (vs. 24) _____ Heaven will be totally pure and free of any evil. There will be *no sin* in God's kingdom; only *those who are saved* will be there. How do you know for sure that you are saved from your sin, that you are a child of God forever? John 1:12 says, "But as many as received Him, to them he gave the right to become children of God, to those who believe in His name." Whose child are you now? _____ He gave you the right (the permission and the power) to become His son or daughter because you received Him, believing in Him. He says in 2 Corinthians 6:18, "I will be a Father to you, and you shall be My sons and daughters, says the LORD Almighty." By the way, when you are a *child of God,* it does <u>not</u> mean you are ever a "little god." There is only one God, who is Christ Jesus.

- **God's Dwelling Place and Promise**

Read **Galatians 4:6-7**. Where is Jesus now? _____ Who has God sent into your heart? _____ The *Spirit of His Son* (Holy Spirit) actually lives *in your heart* now. He is not only in heaven, but inside you, His child! The Holy Spirit is God. Hebrews 13:5c says, "I will never leave you, nor forsake you." It means Jesus will <u>never</u> leave you. Let that sink in.

- **God's Seal**

Look up **John 6:37**. (Keep your finger here.) How many people that come to Jesus are turned away by Him? _____ Will our Father cast out anyone from heaven that comes to Him? _____ This verse says that all people who come to the Lord Jesus have already been chosen by the Father God. It also says this in John 15:16: "You did not choose Me, but I chose You and appointed you that you should go and bear fruit." This means God chose you to become His child and to act like a child of the King (fruit).

Read **John 6:27**. What has the Father set on you? _____ When a king in Bible times would send a letter, it had his seal on it. That proved it was from the king and no one could open it except for the person to whom it was addressed. A seal is a guarantee of a person's word. Just as we have a seal on our birth certificate to prove it is the original birth certificate, God says He will give you everlasting life because He has *sealed* you as His. <u>Circle all words in verses 13-14 that show you are God's child forever</u>. Ephesians 1:13-14 says, "In Him you also trusted, after you heard the word of truth, the gospel of your salvation; in whom also, having believed, you were sealed with the Holy Spirit of promise, who is the guarantee of our inheritance until the redemption of the purchased possession, to the praise of His glory." It is wonderful to know that as a child of God, you are *sealed* by the Holy Spirit, have a *guaranteed* inheritance in heaven, and are His precious *purchased possession!*

DAY 4
Evidence that Reveals a Change: My Beliefs

Memory Verses, Gospel Points, and Spiritual Gifts Profile:

Say the memorization five times or play the erase game.

1. <u>GP3</u>: Jesus, God's only Son, willingly paid for the punishment of your sin through His death, blood, burial, and coming back alive. (1 Corinthians 15:3-4; Hebrews 9:22b; 1 John 1:7b)
   <u>1 John 1:7b</u> "The blood of Jesus Christ His Son cleanses us from all sin."

2. <u>GP4</u>: What would you like for Jesus to do about your sin problem now?
   <u>Romans 10:9 and 13</u>: "That if you confess with your mouth the Lord Jesus and believe in your heart that God has raised Him from the dead, you will be saved." "For whoever calls on the name of the LORD shall be saved."

3. Complete your **Spiritual Gifts Profile.** Turn in at the next meeting.

Lord Jesus, prepare my heart to believe the truths in Your Word today and show me the evidence of my salvation if I am truly Your child. Teach me to discern in love when someone is a real believer or not so I will make the right choices. Give me the strength to live out a changed life for Your glory. In Jesus' name, Amen.

The Evidence

Bank Robbers in Love

There is a story about a man who played professional baseball and ended up on the bench. He became so discouraged that he quit. He could not find a decent job and ended up robbing banks. Of course, he got caught. He went to jail, served a few years, and got out. He could not find a job now that he had a record. So guess what he did? He robbed more banks. He soon met a girl, and they fell in love. She was from a Christian family and knew she should not be dating this bad guy, but she did. He talked her into going on the road with him, robbing banks for about three years, until they finally got caught. Her family found out about her evil life and talked her into turning in herself, hoping for a lighter sentence. Instead, she escaped and went on the road with him again, spending all their bank money. It soon ran out. They were both caught and went to prison for a long time. Numbers 32:23c tells us, "be sure your sin will find you out."

Do you think that young lady was a Christian and was not right with God for a while? She was from a religious family and had been taught right things. If a person is from a Christian family, does it make that person a Christian? Everyone makes mistakes, right? What does God's Word say?

How do we know if there is enough evidence to prove whether a person is a really saved or not? Let's look at the Word of God for answers.

Read **2 Corinthians 5:17.** What happens when we are "in Christ"? _____ _____ What things have "passed away"? _____ How many things have become new? _____ Was there any evidence that proved that the young lady in the story was a new creation? _____ The verse above tells us that once we are in Christ, that is, saved from our sin, we actually become a *new creation.* Our *old way of life* has gone. *All things* become new! A Christian and someone who continues in the old lifestyle cannot be in the same body. When we are true believers, we will change, not only in our beliefs, but also in our desires and behavior. That does not mean our behavior will be perfect. But God's children will not continue in a <u>lifestyle</u> of sin if they are true Christians. When you are born into a family, you will have the characteristics of that family.

Like Father, Like Son

Has anyone ever said this about you or someone in your family? "It is no wonder he acts that way: like father, like son." Children not only look like one or both parents, but they usually have many of their other characteristics too. If you ever needed evidence to prove that you were a child of your parents, similar traits and mannerisms would probably prove it as much as a legal document. When you become God's child, you will possess qualities that are like your Father God too. This is the evidence that shows you are God's child, a Christian.

Are you ready for the truth? Are you willing to take the fruit test? We will be reading the book of First John (the book that is before Second John, not the other book called the Gospel of John). First John is near the back of the New Testament. As you read, imagine you are your own lawyer trying to find the evidence that proves you are a child of God. Think about yourself and see if there is enough evidence to convict you of being a Christian, a child of your Heavenly Father.

As you read the verses listed below, write down the evidence that sticks out to you for each verse. Do as many as you have time for. Make sure you get several under each category. It is more fun the more evidence you gather. It will either give you joy as you discover that you are truly God's child, or an uneasiness if there is a lot more evidence against you. If there is more evidence against you, then talk to your Bible study leader about any questions.

- **Beliefs**—The <u>truths</u> that you know are true according to God's Word down deep in your heart.

Open your Bible to the book of **First John:**

1. **1 John 2:19**: True believers will continue walking with _____.

2. **1 John 2:21-22**: _____ is the Christ, the _____ of God, the One who died for my sins. (Also 1 John 4:14, 4:15, 5:5)

3. **1 John 2:23**: We cannot _____ the Son: we will _____ our belief in Jesus, the Son of God.

4. **1 John 2:20, 27-28**: The Holy Spirit anoints you with understanding and _____ you what you need to know as you abide in His Word. We will want to abide (or spend time) in God's Word and will be motivated to continue because we know Jesus Christ is _____ soon.

5. **1 John 4:2-3**: All who agree that Jesus Christ is come in the _____ is of God.

6. **1 John 4:6**: I can know the spirit of _____ and spirit of _____.

7. **1 John 5:9-13**: We can _____ (vs. 13) for sure that we have eternal life. We have the _____ (vs. 10) of the Holy Spirit inside ourselves to know we are God's children.

Read the answers above to review these beliefs already in your heart. If you are not sure of your answers, look on the next page (Day 4 answers.) Make sure to look up all the verses and put your answers in pencil first.

Day 4 Answers

- **Beliefs** —See the book of First John:

1. 2:19—True believers will continue walking with *Christ Jesus/God*.

2. 2:21-22—*Jesus* is the Christ, the *Son* of God, the One who died for my sins.

3. 2:23—We cannot *deny* the Son: we will *acknowledge (confess or tell)* our belief in Jesus, the Son of God.

4. 2:20, 27-28—The Holy Spirit anoints you with understanding and *teaches* you what you need to know as you abide in His Word. We will want to abide (or spend time) in God's Word and will be motivated to continue because we know Jesus Christ is *coming* soon.

5. 4:2-3—Everyone that agrees that Jesus Christ is come in the *flesh (came to earth, took on human flesh)* is of God.

6. 4:6 – I can know the spirit of *truth* and spirit of *error*.

7. 5:9-13—We can *know* (vs. 13) for sure that we have eternal life. We have the *witness / testimony* (vs. 10) of the Holy Spirit inside ourselves to help us know we are children of God.

Tomorrow, find out more evidence to check out in God's Word and in your heart.

DAY 5

Evidence that Reveals a Change: My Desires and Actions

Memory Verses, Gospel Points, and Spiritual Gifts Profile:

Say memorization five times or play a memory game. See ideas in the appendix.

1. **GP3**: Jesus, God's only Son, willingly paid for the punishment of your sin through His death, blood, burial, and coming back alive. (1 Corinthians 15:3-4; Hebrews 9:22b; 1 John 1:7b)
   1 John 1:7b "The blood of Jesus Christ His Son cleanses us from all sin."

2. **GP4**: What would you like for Jesus to do about your sin problem now?
   Romans 10:9 and 13 - "That if you confess with your mouth the Lord Jesus and believe in your heart that God has raised Him from the dead, you will be saved." "For whoever calls on the name of the LORD shall be saved."

3. Complete your **Spiritual Gifts Profile.** Turn in at the next meeting.

_____

Dear Father, thank You for changing those who are Your children. Reveal to me if my desires have truly changed or not and cause me to be submissive to what Your Word would teach me today. In Jesus' name, Amen.

- **Heart Desires**

Another change that shows evidence of your Christianity will be that you, as a true child of God, will have an immediate heart change. You will have new desires. Find out what those are.

> A true child of God will have an immediate heart change. You will have new desires.

Turn to the book of **First John:**

1. **1 John 2:15-16** –We will lose a desire for the sinful things of this
   _____.

2. **1 John 2:10 and 3:14**—When we _____ others, we are abiding in the light—the truth of God. That means we will want to spend time studying and obeying God's Word because we love Jesus and He stirs us to love others.

3. **1 John 2:3; 5:3** – We will _____ to keep His commands because the love of God is in us. Do you love the world (sinful things) more than God? _____ Do you love others? _____
   Do you have a special bond with true Christians? _____ Do you desire to obey God? _____

40

Now it is time to check and see how your behavior is changing.

- **Behavior: Actions (Fruit)**

A true child of God will act differently. You will produce fruit that shows your life has been changed. Just as an apple tree bears only apples, you will bear fruit that shows you are a Christian—if you are God's child.

1. **1 John 1:8-10**—We will admit when we _____ after becoming God's child because the truth (God's Word and the Holy Spirit) is in us.

2. **1 John 1:9** – We will want to be in a right relationship with our Heavenly Father, so we will _____ our sin (after we become God's children). Then God can hear our prayers.

3. **1 John 2:24**—If God abides (lives) in you, you will also want to spend time with God in His Word. This is called _____ in the Son and in the Father.

4. **1 John 2:29; 3:17-18**—Because we love God and others, we will want to _____ others.

5. **1 John 3:22** – Believers will desire to talk with their Father by _____ Him in prayer. He will have answered prayers because he _____ His commandments and does good _____.

6. **1 John 4:4; 5:4**—If we are truly _____ of God, we will _____ the world (sin.)

If you have been saved, are you willing to confess to God the sins that you have committed since becoming a Christian? _____ As human beings, believers can still sin because they still have a fleshly body, but they also have a new Spirit (the Holy Spirit), so they do not have to be controlled by evil desires any more. This is because God, the Holy Spirit, gives them the power to do right.

> Just as an apple tree bears only apples, you will bear fruit that shows you are a Christian—if you are God's child.

D. New Desires and Actions Test:

1. Do I want to spend time learning God's Word? _____

2. Do I serve God by helping someone else? _____

3. Do I long to talk to my Heavenly Father and do so? _____

4. Am I keeping His commands (most of the time)? _____

5. Do I feel bad when I sin? _____

6. Do I enjoy doing good deeds because I love God and others (not for praise)? _____

7. Did my life change (beliefs, desires, and behavior) since being saved? _____

8. Have I had victory over immoral behavior, dirty mouth, drugs, or any wrong habits? Is my life cleaner now? _____

9. Do I desire to come to church on a regular basis, and am I starting to do so? _____

10. Have I surrendered to Jesus, as my Lord, who is in charge of my life, and want to obey Him? _____

If you answered yes to these questions and have seen that you have new beliefs, new desires, and new behavior, then you are most likely growing as a follower of Christ and displaying evidence of the change in your heart. If you did not answer yes to all of these questions and are not sure of some of the beliefs or do not have new desires and your behavior has not changed at all, then check to see if you have any evidence after becoming a child of God. Talk to your Bible study leader or a pastor on staff at your church. You may want to go back and read over how to be saved and search your heart to see if you really wanted Jesus to be your Lord or just wanted a free ticket to heaven. If you are sure you are a believer in Jesus, but do not see a lot of evidence yet, then you need to keep spending time in God's Word, in prayer, and in being faithful to church services and Sunday School / small group Bible studies. As you continue to spend time with God and godly people, you will grow spiritually and your Christian fruit tree will blossom with much fruit in its season. Find out about the Fruit Test tomorrow.

Now check your answers to the questions from the book of First John in the next section.

Day 5 Answers:

Do NOT look at this section until <u>AFTER</u> you have completed the B. and C. sections.

- **Heart Desires**—See First John:

1. 2:15-16 –We will lose a desire for the sinful things of this <u>world</u>.

2. 2:10 and 3:14—When we <u>love</u> others, we are abiding in the light—the truth of God. That means we will want to spend time studying and obeying God's Word because we love Jesus and He makes us love others.

3. 2:3; 5:3 – We will <u>desire (want)</u> to keep His commands because the love of God will be in us.

- **Behavior—Actions (Fruit)**—See First John:

1. 1:8-10—We will admit when we <u>sin</u> after becoming God's child because the truth (God's Word and the Holy Spirit) is in us.

2. 1:9 – We will want to be in a right relationship with our Heavenly Father, so we will <u>confess (tell God about)</u> our sin (after we become God's children) so God can hear our prayers.

3. 2:24—If God abides (lives) in you, you will also want to spend time with God in His Word. This is called <u>abiding</u> in the Son and in the Father.

4. 2:29; 3:17-18—Because we love God and love others, we will want to <u>help/give to</u> others in need.

5. 3:22 – A Christian will desire to communicate with his or her Father by <u>asking</u> Him in prayer and will have answered prayers because he or she <u>keeps (obeys)</u> His commandments and does good <u>works (deeds)</u>.

6. 4:4; 5:4—If we are truly <u>born</u> of God, we will <u>overcome (have victory over)</u> the world (or sin.)

DAY 6
Evidence that Reveals a Change: The Fruit Test

Say the memorization to someone today or play the erase game. See if you know it by now.

Memory Verses, Gospel Points, and Spiritual Gifts Profile:

1. **GP3**: Jesus, God's only Son, willingly paid for the punishment of your sin through His death, blood, burial, and coming back alive. (1 Corinthians 15:3-4; Hebrews 9:22b; 1 John 1:7b)
   1 John 1:7b "The blood of Jesus Christ His Son cleanses us from all sin."

2. **GP4**: What would you like for Jesus to do about your sin problem now?
   Romans 10:9 and 13 - "That if you confess with your mouth the Lord Jesus and believe in your heart that God has raised Him from the dead, you will be saved." "For whoever calls on the name of the LORD shall be saved."

3. Complete your **Spiritual Gifts Profile.** Turn in at the next meeting.

Heavenly Father, thank You for being so good, kind, and patient as I grow up in Christ and live out the changes You have made in me. Please develop more godly fruit in me so other people can see a difference and be drawn to become Your child. In Jesus' name, Amen.

We have looked at our beliefs, our heart desires, and our behavior as a Christian. That is a lot of evidence so far. But let's take a fruit test and see what happens.

The Fruit Test

We tried to grow a peach tree, but when it finally produced peaches, they were scrawny, had black spots on them, and could not be eaten. The tree never produced peaches again. How do you know if you or others are truly saved from their sins and are going to heaven? You look at the fruit produced in their lives. John 15:8 says, "By this My Father is glorified, that you bear much fruit; so you will be My disciples." When we produce godly attitudes and actions, it will show that we are followers of Jesus, that is, His true disciples. Would the peach tree still be a peach tree if it had never produced any peaches? It could be that it was not really a peach tree, or it may have been a peach tree, but it would be hard to prove it if it never accomplished the purpose for which it was created.

- **What is Spiritual Fruit?** Read the Scriptures in **bold** below to find the answers.

1. **Matthew 5:16** – It is doing _____ works (Isaiah 1:17; Colossians 1:10; 1 Timothy 6:18; Titus 2:7 and 14, 3:8; Hebrews 10:24; James 2:18; 1 Peter 2:12).

2. **Matthew 4:19** – When you follow Jesus, you will help others _____ Him too by leading them to accept Jesus as their Savior, and encouraging them to grow in Jesus by studying and obeying His Word.

3. **John 13:35** – People will know we are disciples (followers) of Jesus when we _____ others.

4. **Galatians 5:22-23** – List the fruits of the Spirit: _____

_____

Spiritual fruit is doing *good works*, helping others *know* Jesus as Savior and Lord, and *loving others*. The fruits of the Spirit are *love, joy, peace, longsuffering (patience or endurance), kindness, goodness, faithfulness, gentleness, self-control (temperance)*. Any of these qualities may show up right away after becoming a Christian, but some attitudes and actions may take years to show up. Just as it takes time for a tree to grow and produce fruit, it also takes time for a new believer to produce many godly qualities. Once you are saved, you will want to serve God and please Him out of a grateful, changed, clean heart.

5. Good deeds are evidence of a changed heart that believes by faith. The Word of God says in Matthew 7:16a, "You will know them by their fruits." A tree that bears delicious, healthy fruit is a good tree, but a bad tree will produce rotten, diseased food or none at all. Real Christians will naturally produce good works. Faith is real when we want to serve Jesus and obey Him. Do not get this concept mixed up. Good works are an evidence of faith <u>after</u> salvation, but not a requirement <u>with</u> faith to become saved. There is a big difference. You must trust Jesus to forgive you of your sin and never trust in any good deeds that you do for your salvation.

6. Read **John 10:27-28.** If you are one of God's sheep, you will <u>desire to follow</u> Jesus, the Good Shepherd. God knows His children, and they will want to follow Him. You know how a little boy just adores his daddy and wants to be just like him? He puts on his shoes and tries to talk and walk like him, doesn't he? We should naturally adore our Heavenly Daddy, too. When we are truly His daughter or son, we will want to follow His commands. That means we will want to learn what His commands are and get to know our Father better by reading and studying His Word. We will desire to please Him. This verse also means that God will never allow you to lose your gift of salvation. Your Father, God, always keeps His promises. He is perfect, unlike earthly parents who may sometimes break promises.

What happens if a believer chooses not to follow the Lord's commands? Having the free gift of salvation does not mean Christians can sin—do anything they want— and get away with it. Not obeying God always brings punishment, sorrow, and consequences. But being a Christian does not mean believers will never do wrong again. We all still have a choice, either to obey God or disobey Him. Before a believer becomes His child, there is no power in anyone to do right. If a non-Christian obeyed the rules, it was only out of selfish reasons such as looking good in front of others, making people like him or her, or not getting in trouble. A non-believer is dead in his or her sins. But once we are saved, we have the Holy Spirit living in us. This empowers God's children with His strength to choose to do right and avoid doing wrong. This shows God is the Heavenly Father of all who are saved. A true Christian will always belong to God. The blood of Jesus has cleansed believers once and for all, making His children God's eternal, adopted, forgiven heirs. Once you are His child, you have the power to do right! You do not have to sin again.

7. If the Holy Spirit is living in you, you will <u>feel bad if you sin</u> and <u>want to be right</u> with your Heavenly Father. Hebrews 13:6b says, "The Lord is my helper." He will help you do right. As you keep studying God's Word, you will have additional strength to do right day after day, and you will be able to decrease sin in your life. But none of us will be totally perfect until we get to heaven. If you choose to disobey the principles in the Bible, then you and your Father, God, cannot be in close fellowship until you make it right. Just as a son needs to say he is sorry and ask forgiveness when he rebels against his father, you need to admit you were wrong and ask forgiveness when you sin against God.

Does a young person lose the privilege of belonging to his parents just because he disobeyed them? No, and God does not disown those of His children who sinned against Him, but they need to apologize and sincerely try to please the Lord. Can a teenager go ask his dad for a gift right after he has broken his rules? _____ In the same way, our Father will not answer a prayer from His son or daughter who is living in disobedience or with unconfessed sin. God is always able to hear our prayers, but because He is a holy God, He cannot look at sin. So if we get our feet dirty spiritually by sinning after we are adopted by Him, He will not hear our prayers until we confess to Him what we have done wrong (Isaiah 59:1-2). He will always listen to a prayer that says you are sorry for your sin. "If we confess our sins, He is faithful and just to forgive us our sins and to cleanse us from all unrighteousness" (I John 1:9). This verse is written to believers who need to make things right sometimes. This verse is not talking about a confession to God when you repented of all sin in order to become saved. This confession is if you sin after you are already adopted by God. If you are saved, you already have a permanent <u>relationship</u> with God as your Father, but now you only need to make right the <u>fellowship</u> between you and Jesus that was broken by your disobedience.

Did you find evidence according to God's Word that shows you are a true Christian? _____ Did you learn anything new that you can share with others? ____ What is the verdict? Are you a fruit-producing Christian? _____ Is there enough evidence to convict you? _____ If you have questions, be sure to talk to your Bible study leader and your pastor.

Let's review what you learned in chapter two.

V. The Greatest Gift

   A. Has God's Love Conquered the Enemy of Sin in Your Life Yet?
   B. Who Must You Believe on to be Saved? The Lord Jesus

VI. Accepting God's Gift

   A. Jesus is the Only Way
   B. The Salvation ABC's
   C. Recording My New Birthday

VII. God's Guarantee

    A. God's Birth Certificate
    B. God's Dwelling Place and Promise
    C. God's Seal

VIII. The Evidence

    A. Beliefs
    B. Heart Desires
    C. Behavior: Actions (Fruit)
    D. New Desires and Actions Test
    E. What is Spiritual Fruit? Fruits of the Spirit, witnessing, obeying God, and more

Thank You, Lord Jesus, for allowing me to accept the greatest gift with You as my Lord and Savior! It is comforting to know that Your free gift to me is guaranteed forever. Help me to live out the evidence of right beliefs from Your Word, to have godly heart desires, and display obedient actions. May the fruit of Your Spirit shine in my heart and life for Your honor and glory. In Jesus' name, Amen.

CHAPTER 3
Look at My Picture -
Who I Am in Christ

DAY 1
Who Am I?

Say memory verses, references, Gospel points, and N. T. books five times each day.

<u>**Memorization and Testimony Worksheet**</u>:

1. <u>**GP5**</u>: Allow Jesus to save you from your sins and change your life. It is as simple as ABC: (Salvation verses: Romans 10:9 and 13 or John 1:12) (Changed life: 2 Corinthians 5:17)
   Admit you are a sinner; ask for forgiveness and repent.
   Believe Jesus died to pay for your sins and came back alive.
   Call on **Jesus'** name (as **Lord**) and tell Him A. and B.

2. <u>**GP6**</u>: Would you like to pray to God to save you now? (If no, give a tract. If yes, ask questions first about ABC's that cannot be answered with a yes or no. If ready, guide them in prayer –ABC's.)

3. <u>**2 Corinthians 5:17**</u> "Therefore, if anyone is in Christ, he is a new creation; old things have passed away; behold, all things have become new."

4. <u>**Testimony worksheet**</u> –Fill out testimony worksheet (Appendix F). Hand in this week.

   Books of the Bible: New Testament: Matthew, Mark, Luke, John, Acts, Romans, 1st and 2nd Corinthians, Galatians…

Dear Heavenly Father, I praise Your name for being such an awesome God! Thank you for changing me into a new creation because of the sacrifice of Your Son, Jesus. Please open my eyes to grasp this truth daily. Help me to walk in victory over sin as a new person with a new life for Your honor and glory. In Jesus' name, Amen.

Who I Am Now – Before and After Pictures

Who Am I?
In the movie *Titanic*, there was a lady from a wealthy family. She enjoyed the prestige and power that came with her family name. She was present at all the events that her upperclass wealthy friends attended. She enjoyed her lavish lifestyle. But one day, she told her daughter some devastating news. She was not who her daughter thought she was. Her mother had changed her name many years ago to appear wealthy. She socialized with the wealthy so they could live a fake life of wealth as long as they could. But the day had come that the truth was coming out if her daughter did not marry a rich man. It could not be hidden any longer, so she agreed to marry him.

Otherwise, they would not have any inheritance, not even their own name. How awful to find out you are not who you thought you were! But being God's child is secure because God tells you who you are in Christ, and how tremendously you are loved.

It reminds us of a married couple who hears the good news that they are going to have a baby. When their precious baby is finally born, their whole world has changed. When you ask Jesus to save you from your sin, you are like a baby who has been born into God's family. Everything about a newborn is new and fresh. Jesus says you have been changed to a new person on the inside.

Let's look at your new picture—the picture that God sees: Here is just a glimpse. Once you are saved, you are a new person, cleansed of sin, with new desires—a new nature, a new peace, a new position, a new family, new abilities, a new spirit, and the potential to become successful in every area of your life! You are on the right road in life. Have you ever asked yourself the question, "Who am I?" Whoever you thought you were before, you can erase it and start all over now. You have a new slate. You are someone great and very special because God has created you in His image.

Have you ever seen the before and after pictures of people when they have lost weight or get a makeover? One can hardly believe it is the same person in some cases. Did you know that you have before and after pictures too? These are pictures that show what happens when we lose our weight of sin. These pictures really show a whole new person. Let's find out all about the new you.

Directions for next section: Read about your condition <u>before</u> you repented and believed in Jesus. Then <u>look up at least one verse telling who you were before</u> and <u>at least one verse telling who you are now</u>. <u>Fill in the blanks</u> that say, "I am ____" and any other blanks to better understand who you are in Christ <u>after</u> you received Jesus Christ into your life. Experience joy in learning about the blessings God gave to you at your salvation. Check your answer by looking at the *italicized* words in each section.

<u>Before Salvation</u>	<u>Who I Am Now In Jesus</u>
(Before Pictures)	**(After Pictures)**

- **I was a Walking, Dead Person**
  (Ephesians 2:1)

- I am a _____
  (2 Corinthians 5:17)

Read **John 11:38-44**—The story of Lazarus. What did Jesus tell the people to do in verse 44? ____ _____ You were a walking, dead person (Eph. 2:1) before you were saved, but you have been resurrected in Christ. This reminds me of Lazarus, when Jesus said, "*Loose him, and let him go.*" He was let go from his grave clothes because Jesus made him come back alive! God changed you into a new person spiritually just as He changed Lazarus in the physical sense. Lazarus' body eventually died again, but his spirit was resurrected when he went to heaven. You will be resurrected someday too!

Did you know that you are like a caterpillar that has turned into a butterfly? God says in His Word, "Therefore, if anyone is in Christ, he is a new creation; old things are passed away; behold, all things have become new" (2 Cor. 5:17). This means you can say, "I have new beliefs, new desires, and will have new behavior. This is because I have the Spirit of God living in me, and my spirit has been reborn. Because *I am a new creature*, I am now dead to sin, but alive to God! I have the power to walk right with God in newness of life. I do not have to do wrong anymore. I can choose to do right. I can choose to disobey God, but I will be disappointed if I do, so I choose God's way!" (Fill in the first blank of who you are in Christ now.)

5. How do you have victory over any sin, such as lying and dishonesty mentioned in this verse? Psalm 120:1-2 says, "In my distress I cried to the LORD, and He heard me. Deliver my soul, O LORD, from lying lips and from a deceitful tongue." _____ _____ When you *call on God in prayer* for help, will He hear you? _____ Since we know God hears the prayers of His children when they call for help to have victory over any wrong habit, then what keeps you from doing that? _____ When I give a Bible to someone, I like to write a quote at the front of it. It says, "This book will keep me from sin, or *sin* will keep me from this book." When you stay in the Word, God will give you strength and a stronger desire to obey Him. Then you will do wrong less and less and obey God more often.

> **I have the power to walk right with God in newness of life. I do not have to sin anymore. I can choose to do right.**

6. Where does your help come from? _____Psalm 121:1-2 says, "I will lift up my eyes to the hills, from whence comes my help? My help comes from the LORD, Who made heaven and earth." Is the *Lord*, the One who helps you, capable of giving you the strength to live victoriously like a new creature? _____ How do you know? What accomplishment did God carry out in the above verse? _____ Do you think that Someone Who *made heaven and earth* is strong enough and wise enough to help you with any problem or struggle you go through? _____ He is over-qualified, and aren't you glad? _____ Remember to cry out to God in prayer and He will help you with your needs! Continue tomorrow finding out more of who you are in Christ—your new picture.

DAY 2
A New Birthday

Say memory verses, references, Gospel points, and N. T. books five times each day.

Memorization and Testimony Worksheet:

1. **GP5:** Allow Jesus to save you from your sins and change your life. It is as simple as ABC: (Salvation verses: Romans 10:9 and 13 or John 1:12) (Changed life: 2 Corinthians 5:17)
   Admit you are a sinner; ask for forgiveness and repent.
   Believe Jesus died to pay for your sins and came back alive.
   Call on **Jesus'** name (as **Lord**) and tell Him A. and B.

2. **GP6:** Would you like to pray to God to save you now? (If no, give a tract. If yes, ask questions first about ABC's that cannot be answered with a yes or no. If ready, guide them in prayer –ABC's.)

3. **2 Corinthians 5:17** "Therefore, if anyone is in Christ, he is a new creation; old things have passed away; behold, all things have become new."

4. **Testimony worksheet** –Fill out testimony worksheet (Appendix F). Hand in this week.

   Books of the Bible: New Testament: Matthew, Mark, Luke, John, Acts, Romans, 1st and 2nd Corinthians, Galatians…

Lord Jesus, thank You for being a God who allows me to start over with a new birthday in Your family. Please help me to comprehend more great truths today of who I am now because of Your wonderful gift of salvation. In Jesus' name, Amen.

A Birth Miracle

Before our son's birth, I had fallen on my stomach in the ninth month. I prayed earnestly to God that He would protect my baby and me. The doctors stopped any possibility of labor that night; a few weeks later, it was time for him to be born. I did not know that during my labor my blood pressure had dropped so low that I became unconscious. My husband happened to see the doctor bumping his head against the wall, not knowing what to do because he knew I could lose my life and the baby's life. Finally he gave me some medicine that brought my blood pressure up, and I gave birth to our son. We were happy to have a son, but we did not hear him crying. I started to be concerned and prayed for him to breathe. In a few minutes, what seemed like a long time, I heard the precious cry of our son. He was fine! The doctor saw evidence that I had been bleeding internally, and somehow the bleeding had been stopped. Our baby had a double knot in his cord which could have meant he did not have enough oxygen to live or could be brain damaged. But he is alive today and very smart making A's and B's in school. God produced many miracles in the birth of our son! We thanked God for answered prayer and for both our lives. Just as God produced miracles in the physical birth of our son, He also produces a miracle when we are born into His family. Read the story of Nicodemus and find out about the miracle of your spiritual birth.

- **I was Born—Only Physically
  An Incomplete Person**
  (John 3:3)

- **I am** _____ _____
  and C_____ **in in Christ.**
  (Colossians 2:10)

Read **John 3:1-8** – The story of Nicodemus. What did Jesus say (vs. 3 and 7) had to happen for anyone to see the kingdom of God? _____ First we are born of water, literally like rain water (vs. 5), that is, a physical birth like a baby born from a sac of water. This water is compared to our flesh in verse 6. "Flesh" means our body as in skin or human. Jesus is helping him understand that we are born first physically, but then we also must be born again—spiritually. Spiritual birth occurs when God's Spirit comes to live in us when we ask Him to come and save us. This filling of the Holy Spirit is not a baptism of water. Jesus emphasizes *a person must be born again* by believing in Jesus (verses 16-18 and 36). Jesus made sure Nicodemus knew what he needed to know to see the kingdom of God. What was it? It was what happened to you. You can say now, "*I am born again!*"

Colossians 2:10 says, "And you are complete in Him, who is the head of all principality and power." What do you think "complete" means? _____ _____ _____Some of the words that describe it in the Greek are "finish," "verify," "complete," "fill up," "full," "perfect." In other words, you are a finished, complete, perfectly verified child of God now. You are in possession of all things from God necessary for your spiritual maturity. There is no need to add any good works to gain your salvation. Jesus already did all the work for you and you are completely saved because of Christ's work on the cross. Before salvation, you were dead spiritually, but alive physically. Now you are alive physically and spiritually! Continue to choose to be dead to sin every day as you choose to obey Christ. Christ makes you *complete as in oneness in marriage*. Now you can say, "*I am complete in Christ!*"

- **I was Sentenced to Hell.**

  (John 3:36 and Revelation 20:15)

- **I am** _____ **and** _____
  _____ .
  (Romans 10:13; John 6:37; Ephesians 1:13-14; John 3:16)

Have you heard of the people who were saved from the Twin Towers in New York City on September 11, 2001? They were delivered from a physical death. They were protected from having their lives destroyed by the awful actions of terrorists. How thankful they must be for having their lives saved! On the other hand, how sad for those precious people who were victims of that evil act. But all Christians who have believed in Jesus Christ and His resurrection (for their sin) have been saved from a greater destruction. As unsaved people, we would have been doomed forever to suffer the consequences of God's wrath on sin in a burning hell. A physical death will never be the end for us, only the beginning of eternity to spend with Jesus. After salvation, you are saved from the punishment for your sin. Praise God! *"Saved"* in the Greek (sozo) means to "deliver or protect, heal, preserve, save, do well, be whole." When you are saved, this means God has preserved your soul for heaven, protected you from being punished for your sins in hell, and healed you from your sin disease, making you totally, spiritually well and whole! (Other verses to study are Luke 7:50; John 3:17; and 10:9; Acts 16:31; Ephesians 2:8 and 9.)

1. John 3:36 says, "He who believes in the Son has everlasting life; and he who does not believe the Son shall not see life, but the wrath of God abides on him." What happens to the person that does not believe in the Son of God (Jesus)? _____

   _____

"Wrath" means "punishment, anger, indignation, vengeance." Those who do not believe Jesus is God's Son by trusting Him for their salvation *will not see everlasting life* in heaven, but *God's wrath will be on the person who rejects Jesus' gift* of forgiveness. His wrath must punish all evil. God hates it when people break His laws because He is holy (perfect) and without any wickedness. But He loves the sinner.

Revelation 20:15 says, "And anyone not found written in the Book of Life was cast into the lake of fire." When you are saved, God writes your name in a special book called the Book of Life in heaven as a record of your spiritual birth. This happened the moment you prayed to ask forgiveness of your sins, when you believed Jesus died and arose for you, making Him Lord. Those who have not asked Jesus for forgiveness or believed in Him are condemned to be punished in the lake of fire (hell) by their own choice (John 3:17-18).

God has already done everything in His power to save the world. It is up to each person to accept His gift. It is our job to pray for our friends and family and tell them how to accept God's gift of eternal life by being born again. (Other verses to look up about the Book of Life are Luke 10:20; Philippians 4:3; Hebrews 12:23; Revelation 3:5, 13:8, 20:12, 21:27, and 22:19.)

2. Read **Ephesians 1:13-14**. Jesus saved you when you trusted in Him by believing the Gospel, and He sealed you by putting the Holy Spirit in you. What word proves that you have an inheritance as His child (vs. 14)? _____

Did you know that God *guaranteed* you were His child just like someone who puts down earnest money on a purchase? He promised you through the Holy Spirit, and it is just like a down payment on an engagement ring. Nothing will separate you from His love (Romans 8:35-39). He always keeps His promises. Now you can say, *"I am saved and guaranteed eternity!"* I have a new birthday in God's family and a new home in heaven. (Remember to fill in the blanks of who you are now.)

A Surprise Announcement

Try playing a game today to help with your memorization. See Appendix B.

Memorization and Testimony Worksheet:

1. **GP5:** Allow Jesus to save you from your sins and change your life. It is as simple as ABC: (Salvation verses: Romans 10:9 and 13 or John 1:12) (Changed life: 2 Corinthians 5:17)
   Admit you are a sinner; ask for forgiveness and repent.
   Believe Jesus died to pay for your sins and came back alive.
   Call on **Jesus'** name (as **Lord**) and tell Him A. and B.

2. **GP6:** Would you like to pray to God to save you now? (If no, give a tract. If yes, ask questions first about ABC's that cannot be answered with a yes or no. If ready, guide them in prayer –ABC's.)

3. **2 Corinthians 5:17** "Therefore, if anyone is in Christ, he is a new creation; old things have passed away; behold, all things have become new."

4. **Testimony worksheet** –Fill out testimony worksheet (Appendix F). Hand in this week.

   Books of the Bible: New Testament: Matthew, Mark, Luke, John, Acts, Romans, 1st and 2nd Corinthians, Galatians…

Jesus, thank You for not looking at me as Your enemy anymore. Show me how to grasp the magnitude of who You have changed me to be. I am thankful for my new relationship with You! In Jesus' name, Amen.

- **I was an Enemy of God**
  (Romans 5:10)

- **I am now God's** _____.
  (John 15:15)

Corrie Ten Boom was an amazing lady. She and her family were sent to a concentration camp because they hid Jewish people in their home during a time when Hitler was killing the Jews. This family showed their love for God and others by protecting His chosen people. If you have ever read her books, you know that all of her family died, but she finally got out of the awful, dirty concentration camp alive. There came a time later when she ran into one of the concentration camp guards. He was living out in society also. Her flesh wanted to hate him for what he had done to her and her family. But she chose to obey God and love this man as a person who needed God to forgive him of his sins. Jesus gave her the strength to replace hate with love for those who hurt her.

Corrie Ten Boom said, "Even as the angry, vengeful thoughts boiled through me, I saw the sin of them. Jesus Christ had died for this man; was I going to ask for more? 'Lord Jesus,' I prayed, 'forgive me and help me to forgive him... Jesus, I cannot forgive him. Give me Your forgiveness.' And so I discovered that it is not on our forgiveness any more than on our goodness that the world's healing hinges, but on His. When he tells us to love our enemies, he gives along with the command, the love itself."[1]

1. Could you ever love those who hurt you? _____ We must understand that we are not to be enemies with others, only Satan. "For we do not wrestle against flesh and blood, but against principalities, against powers, against the rulers of the darkness of this age, against spiritual hosts of wickedness in the heavenly places" (Ephesians 6:12). The Word of God says that you and I can say, "I can do all things through Christ who strengthens me" (Philippians 4:13). To forgive someone, separate the sin from the person. That is how God chooses to forgive us all. He chooses to love us, but

> **To forgive someone, separate the sin from the person.**

He does not love our sin. None of us can love those who hurt us without God's strength in us. You can choose to have compassion on the person who hurt you, but still hate the sin that person committed. When you love the person with God's love, you will give him or her over to God and pray for him or her. You can then forgive. Forgiveness is not excusing the sin, just turning the person over to God for Him to deal with him or her. Then do not worry about it and harbor any bitterness. You may even be able to be friends again if the person is willing to repent of the sin toward you.

Matthew 19:26 says, "But Jesus looked at them and said to them, 'With men this is impossible, but with God all things are possible.'"

Romans 5:10 says, "For if when we were enemies we were reconciled to God through the death of His Son, much more, having been reconciled, we shall be saved by His life."

2. What relationship did we have with God when He decided to save us? _____ When you were His *enemy* because of your sin, God gave His Son Jesus to die in your place. Not only did He love you when you were His enemy, but He started a new relationship with you.

3. Read **John 15:15**. What does God call you now? _____ You are a specially chosen, very much loved, and appreciated friend of God Almighty. How does God show you that you are His friend and not just a servant according to verse 15? _____
_____

Friends communicate with one another and share each other's secrets, plans, joys, and burdens. Jesus communicates with you through His Word the Bible and through His Spirit and your spirit. God is eager to talk to you and for you to talk to Him. He is kind and approachable and wants to share His heart with you. He desires to hear your burdens, joys, plans, and all the thoughts of your heart because He is your friend! *He tells us all things* from God the Father. Do you feel special? Now you can say, *"I am now God's friend!"*

- **I was not Aware of How Much I was Loved.**

- **I am** _____ _____
  _____.
  (John 15:9; Jeremiah 31:3; Romans 8:35-39)

1. Have you ever known someone that did not know how to love others? This could possibly happen if a person was never shown true love from anyone. Read **John 15:9.** Who loved Jesus? _____ Because Jesus was loved perfectly by *His Father, God*, and because He is also God, He can love you perfectly without any conditions attached. As imperfect humans, we tend to love others conditionally. We may think we love another person if these criteria are available: "They treat me great;" "they help me when I need them;" or "they look attractive." But we should love others unconditionally as God loves us. This is love that is not dependent on one's actions or looks, but instead it chooses to love regardless of circumstances. Which way does God love you? _____ Did you do anything to make Jesus love you? _____ Are you glad that God loves you with perfect love, and not with any strings attached? _____

2. Jeremiah 31:3b says, "Yes, I have loved you with an everlasting love; Therefore with lovingkindness I have drawn you." How long will God love you? _____ Does His love depend on what you say or do or on any sins you commit? _____ Is it wonderful to be loved *forever* and so perfectly? _____

3. Read **Romans 8:35-39** again if you like. Nothing can separate you from God's love for you. Now you can say, "*I am loved unconditionally forever!*"

Find out tomorrow about more blessings of who you are in Christ Jesus. (Fill in the last two blanks of who you are now).

A Surprise Inheritance

Say memory verses, references, Gospel points, and N. T. books five times each day.

Memorization and Testimony Worksheet:

1. **GP5:** Allow Jesus to save you from your sins and change your life. It is as simple as ABC: (Salvation verses: Romans 10:9 and 13 or John 1:12) (Changed life: 2 Corinthians 5:17) **A**dmit you are a sinner; ask for forgiveness and repent. **B**elieve Jesus died to pay for your sins and came back alive. **C**all on **Jesus'** name (as **Lord**) and tell Him A. and B.

2. **GP6:** Would you like to pray to God to save you now? (If no, give a tract. If yes, ask questions first about ABC's that cannot be answered with a yes or no. If ready, guide them in prayer –ABC's.)

3. **2 Corinthians 5:17** "Therefore, if anyone is in Christ, he is a new creation; old things have passed away; behold, all things have become new."

4. **Testimony worksheet** –Fill out testimony worksheet (Appendix F). Hand in this week.

   Books of the Bible: New Testament: Matthew, Mark, Luke, John, Acts, Romans, 1st and 2nd Corinthians, Galatians…

Dear Father God, thank You for Your perfect love for me. Help my heart and mind to be cleansed and to be open to the wonderful truths in Your Word and how much my inheritance has changed since becoming a part of Your family! In Jesus' name, Amen.

- **I was a Child of the Devil**
  (John 8:44)

- I am a _____
  _____
  (John 1:12; Ephesians 1:5; 2 Corinthians 6:18)

1. Read the Gospel of **John 1:12**. When you believe on Jesus' name, what do you have the right (permission or power) to become? _____ When you believe on Jesus' name and that He alone will save you, then you have the right or power from God's authority to become (son or daughter, prince or princess) *a child of God*.

Adopted Daughter

We know a sweet girl whom we will call Annie, who is from the Ukraine. Annie had a mother who left her and a father who traveled the world too busy to take responsibility for his only daughter. So Annie had to live with her grandparents. The grandfather soon died, and the grandmother was so poor she could not continue to take care of Annie. Annie did not have enough food to eat at her house. An added problem was that the grandmother developed a disease and knew she would die soon. So she placed Annie in an orphanage. Annie lived there a few years, and one day was adopted by a very kind single lady. Annie became her daughter, and soon this lady married a nice young man who also adopted her as his daughter. Annie's eyes sparkle now because she is loved and specially chosen when no one else could take care of her and give her the love she needed. God says, "When my father and my mother forsake me, then the LORD will take care of me" (Psalm 27:10). The Lord Jesus will take care of His children, one way or another. Are you glad He loved you that much? _____

2. Read **Ephesians 1:5.** What is it called when parents choose a child to become their own? _____ God chose you for the purpose of adopting you as His child. *Adoption* by Almighty God shows He has accepted you because of Jesus Christ. You are unconditionally loved by God, your perfect Heavenly Father. John 15:16 says, "You did not choose Me, but I chose you and appointed you that you should go and bear fruit, and that your fruit should remain, that whatever you ask the Father in My name He may give you." God chose you for a very important purpose. He knew you would have great potential. Why did God choose you to receive His blessings according to the above verse? _____

You were chosen to become God's child because He loves you but also to fulfill God's purpose so you could *go and bear fruit.* How does a Christian bear fruit? Answer that by answering this question: What is a fruit tree's purpose? _____ You have a very important purpose too. You will learn how to *bear fruit,* that is, to become more and more like Christ as you grow closer to God by reading His Word daily. As you continue to spend time with God and be faithful in church and small group Bible study, you will become more loving, joyful, peaceful, patient, kind, and strong in many ways. Will it be easy? No. But anything with great results and rewards takes time and patience and an attitude of not giving up. You can do all things through Christ strengthening you. You will even learn how to reproduce yourself spiritually by leading other people to Christ. Now that's producing fruit. And as you produce fruit, that is, reproduce little Christs, you will be given *answers to your prayers* too. That means learning what is best for you in God's timing, either a yes, a no, or wait. You cannot fail when you do things God's way. (Other verses to study are 2 Cor. 6:18; Gal. 4:5-7; Rev. 17:14 and Moses starting in Exodus Chapter 2.) Now you can say, "*I am a child of God, adopted by Him as my Heavenly Father!*"

- **I was Under the Control of the Prince of the Power of the Air—the Devil.**
  (Ephesians 2:2)

- I am _____. _____ _____
  _____
  (Revelation 19:16; Psalm 10:16a)

From Rags to Riches

There is a true story told about a boy named Rick who lived in a poor family. He did not have a father and was reared by his mother, who worked the best she could while raising three boys by herself. One day she came home and told her boys she had met a man that would be their new father. She would be married to him, and they would all move to their new house. They would not only have a new daddy, but this father was rich. They would be adopted by him and have just about anything they desired. Of course, the boys were all excited. A new life awaited them. Sure enough, the day came when their mother was married to a rich new daddy. Their new house was bigger than they had ever seen before. But they had another surprise. They had a new big brother, too, and he had bought three new bikes for his three new little brothers. This seemed too good to be true, but it was really happening to them. Their lives changed, not because they had done anything great to deserve it, but because they were willing to be adopted and accept this new daddy who had a new home and a new life for them. This new family was the father of Elvis Presley, and the new big brother was Elvis Presley, the "King of Rock and Roll."[2]

This story reminds me of how we are adopted by a greater Father who has a mansion waiting for us in Heaven and has promised to supply all our needs on earth. We do not deserve it, but it is ours with all the privileges of a prince or princess of the King of kings. Nothing can separate us from His love!

1. Revelation 19:16 says, "And He has on His robe and on His thigh a name written: KING OF KINGS AND LORD OF LORDS." What is God's title in this verse? _____
    _____ It is really special to be a ruler, but to be over all kings and presidents everywhere is as high a position as anyone can attain. God our Father is the *King of kings and Lord of lords*! Psalm 10:16a says, *"The LORD is King forever and ever."* How long will God have this title? _____ Is it comforting to know that your Father in Heaven will *always* be in the highest position of authority? This means you will never lose your position as His royal child. The blessings of who you are in Christ just keep getting better and better.

2. Read **Ephesians 2:6.** Where has Christ allowed you to sit as His royal child? _____
    What a privilege to be seated with Christ in the *heavenly places*. You can sit and reign with the King of all kings someday. If you are to be seated with our supreme King in heaven someday and you are His child, then what does that make you? _____
    You are part of the family of the God, of *royal blood*. Look in Ephesians 2:2. Where did you walk in the past? _____
    We started out with a lousy heritage, walking *in the world in disobedience*. We were children of the devil, the one who rules this world and space. But just like the boy Rick in the true story above, if you have been saved, you now have a new Father. You can now say, *"I am royalty. The King of kings is my Father!"* (Fill in the last two "I am _____" blanks.)

DAY 5
Look at You Now

Say memory verses, references, Gospel points, and N. T. books five times each day.

<u>**Memorization and Testimony Worksheet**</u>:

1. <u>**GP5:**</u> Allow Jesus to save you from your sins and change your life. It is as simple as ABC: (Salvation verses: Romans 10:9 and 13 or John 1:12) (Changed life: 2 Corinthians 5:17)
   Admit you are a sinner; ask for forgiveness and repent.
   Believe Jesus died to pay for your sins and came back alive.
   Call on **Jesus'** name (as **Lord**) and tell Him A. and B.

2. <u>**GP6:**</u> Would you like to pray to God to save you now? (If no, give a tract. If yes, ask questions first about ABC's that cannot be answered with a yes or no. If ready, guide them in prayer –ABC's.)

3. <u>**2 Corinthians 5:17:**</u> "Therefore, if anyone is in Christ, he is a new creation; old things have passed away; behold, all things have become new."

4. <u>**Testimony worksheet:**</u> Fill out testimony worksheet (Appendix F). Hand in this week.

   <u>**Books of the Bible**</u>: New Testament: Matthew, Mark, Luke, John, Acts, Romans, 1st and 2nd Corinthians, Galatians.

Lord Jesus, may You be honored today as I worship You. Please cleanse me of any sin and open my heart to experience joy in how special You have made me. Show me how to live out who I am now and in the future! In Jesus' name, Amen.

- **I was an Alien, a Stranger, Without Christ or Hope**
  (Ephesians 2:12)

- I am a C_____ G_____,
  a R_____ P_____, a
  H_____ N_____,
  and His own S_____ P_____.
  (1 Peter 2:9-10)

1. Read **Ephesians 2:12**. What were you called before you knew Jesus personally as your Father, Lord, King, and Savior? _____

Real Aliens

People have been wondering for years if there is life on other planets. There are all kinds of stories of people being captured by aliens and surviving to tell about their experiences. But there is a true story of life beyond earth, and it is not Mars. It is heaven. If there are aliens, we seriously doubt. But one thing is for sure, we were *aliens and strangers* before we knew Jesus. But we are not talking about little green men. "Aliens" in this verse means a "non-participant." That means before you asked Jesus to forgive you of your sins and believed in His resurrection and accepted His gift of eternal life, you were not a participant in God's promise of eternal life. Read the verse again.

2. What two things were you without? _____
    You do not have to be *without Christ, without God* the Father, or *have no hope*. Now you can say "I have hope in the promise of life forever beyond earth. I am going to be with God in Heaven someday, and He is with me on earth every day until then."

3. Read **Ephesians 1:3-6.** These verses cause us to well up with joy! God has given us "every spiritual blessing." See if you can find at least five of the seven blessings mentioned in these verses.
    1.) _____ 2.) _____ 3.) _____
    4.) _____ 5.) _____

When Jesus *chose you* before the world was formed, that was a special blessing. He made you *holy* (clean and without sin) like Jesus when you were cleansed with His blood at salvation. He looks at you and does *not blame any sin on your account*. It has been paid for by Jesus' blood. He chose you, *adopted* you as His child, and planned your life to be blessed to fulfill a special purpose. Your purpose is meant to go along with *His perfect will or plan*. If you follow God's ways, you will accomplish that purpose and bring *glory and praise to God and be a testimony of His grace* in your life. He calls you "Beloved," meaning you are truly *accepted* and loved by Him!

4. Read **1 Peter 2:9-10.** What are four things that God says you are now? _____
    _____

The Israelites (Jewish people) are God's chosen people. God allowed them to hear about the true God first. But they rejected Jesus Christ, the Messiah. Then God allowed Gentiles to be adopted or grafted into His chosen family. He loves His spiritually adopted children just as much as He loves the nation of Israel. So now all saved people can say we are a *chosen generation* along with the nation of Israel!

You have already learned that you are royalty, but did you know that you are *a royal priest* (Hebrews 7:25-27; Revelation 20:6)? Do not be afraid of that title. You do not have to live perfectly to be God's priest. He already sees you as perfect because of the blood of Christ that covers your sin. He expects you to share Jesus with others and help them grow closer to God as a priest would do. We need to witness daily with our words and lives no matter what our job is on earth. When opportunities come up for you to share Christ (during lunch or a break, at school or wherever you are), be careful you do not neglect your responsibilities at work as you share about what Jesus has done for you. We always want to practice doing right while we speak of the One who can make us right with God. Being God's priest is a lifetime job and a privileged responsibility that should never be neglected.

You are also part of the *holy nation* of God's people. The holy nation is really a mixture of all nations on earth, made up of people who believe in Jesus, the risen Son of God, and who have called on Him to cleanse them from their sins. So you and I should naturally love all Christians no matter what their race, class, age, sex, or position of authority. *His own "special people"* does not mean you are a strange person now. It means you are a "preserved" and "purchased possession." To sum it up, you are a special, prized, purchased possession, one who is valuable, and obtained by God to be preserved for a special purpose!

5. See **1 Peter 2:9-10** again. What purpose did God have in choosing you? _____
    What has He called you out of and into? _____
    What were you before? _____
    Who are you now? _____

A king must be praised because of who he is. God is the King of all kings who chose you to praise Him. Psalm 33:1 says, "Rejoice in the LORD, O you righteous! For praise from the upright is beautiful." You were created *to praise God.* He also says in John 12:32, "And I, if I am lifted up from the earth, will draw all peoples to Myself." That means when you brag on the qualities of Christ, what He has done for you, and what He can do for your friends, people will naturally be drawn to accept Jesus as their God and Father. Do you tell people when Jesus answered your prayers, helped you solve a problem, or showed love to you or your family during the day? _____ These are ways to "lift up Christ" in front of others.

If you were stuck in a dark, old building which was about to cave in and someone called out to you so he or she could rescue you to bring you into the light, would you be grateful? _____ God has rescued you from something much worse than an awful destruction of a collapsed building! He has called you *out of the darkness of sin*, when you were on your way to hell. You are now able to walk *in the marvelous light of God's Word* and know of His love and many blessings. Before, you were *not a part of a true nation of people spiritually, but now you are a holy nation with the people of God.* Before, you had *not been shown mercy*, but *now you have experienced the mercy of forgiveness* for your sins and all of the privileges that go with that blessing. Now you can say, "*I am a chosen generation, a royal priest, a holy nation, a special people!*" (Fill out the blank at the beginning, "I am __".)

DAY 6
A New Record

See how much memorization you know today. Try writing it from memory. Then practice.

Memorization and Testimony Worksheet:

1. **GP5:** Allow Jesus to save you from your sins and change your life. It is as simple as ABC: (Salvation verses: Romans 10:9 and 13 or John 1:12) (Changed life: 2 Corinthians 5:17)
   Admit you are a sinner; ask for forgiveness and repent.
   Believe Jesus died to pay for your sins and came back alive.
   Call on **Jesus'** name (as **Lord**) and tell Him A. and B.

2. **GP6:** Would you like to pray to God to save you now? (If no, give a tract. If yes, ask questions first about ABC's that cannot be answered with a yes or no. If ready, guide them in prayer –ABC's.)

3. **2 Corinthians 5:17:** "Therefore, if anyone is in Christ, he is a new creation; old things have passed away; behold, all things have become new."

4. **Testimony worksheet** –Fill out testimony worksheet (Appendix F). Hand in this week.

   Books of the Bible: New Testament: Matthew, Mark, Luke, John, Acts, Romans, 1st and 2nd Corinthians, Galatians…

Dear Lord Jesus, thank You for loving all of us unconditionally and always handling everything just right. Open my heart to understand and apply Your Word today. Cause me to see who I am through Your lenses of the new record You have created about me. In Jesus' name, Amen.

A Dream Come True

There is a story of a man who wanted to help his country by protecting hidden treasures that were valuable parts of his country's history. Although he had good intentions, he went about it in the wrong way and broke into some of the forbidden buildings that held these historical artifacts. An evil man was after him, who only wanted to steal these valuable treasures to become rich. The story ends with the patriotic man finding the famous historical artifacts and the evil man going to prison. Even though the man who discovered the treasures had good intentions, he still deserved prison. But he got a break because the government wanted to know the location of the treasures to put them in protected museums. So they made a deal with him. If he would give them the location of the treasures and give all artifacts to his country, they would erase his criminal record and count him innocent. He would receive a new, clean record. In addition, they would give him enough money to live like a rich man the rest of his life and be protected from serving any prison sentence. Does this sound too good to be true? That's because it is. It's from the movie *National Treasure*. It is too good to be true on earth. But this story is similar to what happens to all believers spiritually after salvation. Let's find out more.

- **I was Condemned.**
  (John 3:18)

- **I am** _____
  (Romans 5:1 and 18; Romans 3:28)

1. Read **Matthew 27:15-26.** Who was the substitute for Barabbas? _____ Was *Jesus* a thief? _____ Did Jesus do anything to deserve to become a criminal and die a criminal's death? _____ Barabbas is a picture of whom? _____ The thief Barabbas is a picture of *you and all people* ever born because we are all born with the sin curse (Rom. 5:12). But you say, "I am not a thief." You may not be a thief in one sense, but any time a law is broken, that person becomes a lawbreaker. That crime requires punishment. Each time you sin, you are breaking God's law. A child who steals a piece of candy is just as much a thief as a man who embezzles millions of dollars from a company. A person who jokingly tells a "little white lie" is breaking God's law as much as a person who lies on income tax forms. There is no such thing as a white lie or a very bad lie in God's eyes. Yes, some evil deeds get treated with greater punishment in our society. For example, taking a life or blaspheming the Holy Spirit or committing adultery are very serious sins with terrible consequences. But there is no sin greater than another in the light of "the wages of sin is death." Sin is still sin, any way you slice it. Dirt is dirty, whether it is a little or a lot. Before, when our iniquity was not justified or erased and declared perfect in God's eyes, we were guilty and could not be in God's presence ever. We deserved hell and had no hope. But thank God, when you accepted Him as your substitute, you were justified and allowed to be free and perfect in His eyes! "Justified" means to be declared innocent before God. It is to be free of punishment or be declared righteous. That means it is "just as if you have never sinned" in the eyes of the judge. How wonderful!

Romans 5:1 says, "Therefore, having been justified by faith, we have peace with God through our Lord Jesus Christ." Romans 5:18 tells us, "Therefore, as through one man's offense judgment came to all men, resulting in condemnation, even so through one Man's righteous act the free gift came to all men, resulting in justification of life."

2. Remember that being justified is God's declaration that the believing sinner becomes righteous and acceptable before him at the moment of salvation. According to **Romans 5:1 and 18,** how are we justified? _____ What do we receive as a result of being justified? _____ When we have *faith* in what Jesus did on the cross and His resurrection, we have *peace* with God. We can never have peace with a holy God without our sin being justified. Just as Barabbas was made free of the punishment for his crime when Jesus took his place on the cross, so were you. If you have accepted Jesus as your substitute, then you can now say, "*I am justified.*" Remember that "justified" means to be declared innocent before God. It is to be free of punishment or be declared righteous. That means it is "just as if you have never sinned" in the eyes of the judge. Thank You, Jesus, for this good news! (Fill in the "I am" blank.)

3. Read more good news. The Biblical character Moses is another picture of what has happened to you at salvation (Exodus 1-2). (The following references to verses need not be looked up now unless you have extra time. They are references to back up the points being made with God's Word.)

a) (Exodus 1:22, 2:5-10) Even though Moses was supposed to die because of Pharaoh's order to kill all Hebrew baby boys at that time, he lived because of the mercy of Pharaoh's daughter. You deserved to die an eternal death and be punished for your sins, but Jesus, the Son of God and the King of kings, had mercy on you and paid for your adoption with His blood and <u>saved</u> your life (John 1:12; Hebrews 7:25-27, 9:12, 22; 1 John 1:9)!

b) Moses was specially chosen by the King's daughter and loved unconditionally. You have been specially <u>chosen</u> by God and loved unconditionally, forever (Jeremiah 31:3; John 15:16).

c) He was adopted into a royal family, and you have also been <u>adopted</u> into the royal family of believers with God as your King and Father (Romans 8:15; 2 Corinthians 6:18; Galatians 4:5-6; Deuteronomy 14:2; Isaiah 63:16).

d) Moses could have been the next Pharaoh, but God had a greater plan. Moses would lead the children of Israel out of slavery and into their promised land. God also has a wonderful plan for your life as His <u>royal child</u>. As you study God's Word, He will reveal the specifics of that plan in detail. But we do know His plan for all Christians. It is to glorify Him by producing fruit for God's kingdom (Jeremiah 29:11; Acts 26:16; 1 John 3:8; John 15; Matthew 4:16; 1 Corinthians 6:20; 1 Peter 4:11; 2 Peter 1:3-10).

Just think: God could use you to help rescue many people from the slavery of sin and lead them to the promised land of heaven! Are you excited about that? If not, what is hindering your joy?

> * Is it a fear of not knowing what to say? _____
> * Is it hard to imagine another person's eternal destiny as hell? _____
> * Is it too easy to have worldly priorities? _____

Will you determine to obey God so you can glorify Him and fulfill your purpose? _____ Will you be willing to get out of your comfort zone and tell others about Jesus so they can be saved from sin as you have been, even if it seems hard at first? _____ Moses was afraid, but God used him to do something great when he was willing to obey Him. Read the story of Moses starting in Exodus 2 when you have time. It will bless your life. Find out about your birthday gifts next week.

CHAPTER 4

Birthday Gifts –
What I Have in Christ

The Gift of Forgiveness

<u>Memorization:</u> Say the memory verses, references, and Books of the Bible five times.

1. <u>**Ephesians 1:3**</u> "Blessed be the God and Father of our Lord Jesus Christ, who has blessed us with every spiritual blessing in the heavenly places in Christ."

2. <u>**1 John 5:4**</u> "For whatever is born of God overcomes the world. And this is the victory that has overcome the world—our faith."

3. <u>**Hebrews 13:5b and 6a**</u> "I will never leave you nor forsake you. ...The LORD is my helper."

   <u>**Books of the Bible**</u>: (New Testament continued) Galatians, Ephesians, Philippians, Colossians, 1 and 2 Thessalonians, 1 and 2 Timothy, Titus...

Lord Jesus, thank You for being so patient, kind, and forgiving. Please cleanse me of any preconceived ideas on what forgiveness means. Help me to more fully comprehend how much You forgave me and learn to have the strength to forgive others. In Jesus' name, Amen.

A Heavy Burden

Have you ever had to carry a very heavy box or suitcase and there was nobody around to help you? Did your muscles ache continually without any relief? We flew into the Atlanta airport recently and picked up our luggage from baggage claim. We had to hurry from one end of that very large airport to the other. It was so hard carrying everything. But my kind husband saw how I was struggling and took one of my suitcases and piled it onto his load. It was such a relief, and my pain went away instantly. Just as it is a huge relief when someone helps you when you have a physical need, it is even more wonderful when a spiritual burden is lifted. Read how God came to your rescue when He lifted your burden of sin.

Look up the verses below.

- **I was Guilty of Sin.**
  (Romans 5:8)

- **I am** _____.
  (Colossians 2:13; 1 John 2:12)

1. Psalm 32:1 says, "Blessed is he whose transgression is forgiven, whose sin is covered." How are you blessed according to this verse? _____

When your *transgression is forgiven or covered*, that is talking about when you broke God's law by committing wrong deeds or thoughts. Forgiveness is when God actually lifted the huge burden of sin off of you and put it on Jesus. He actually covered your transgressions with His blood. That means your sin is completely removed, gone forever! That is why He could forgive you. What do you think the word "forgive" means?_____

_____

_____

Webster's Dictionary says the word "forgive" means "to *give up resentment against or the desire to punish*; stop being angry with; pardon; to give up all claim to punish or exact penalty for an offense; overlook; to cancel or remit a debt."[1] God truly forgave you when He cancelled your debt you could not pay and gave you a gift you did not deserve. He even chose not to remember your sin after you asked for forgiveness. Would it be nice if we could forget what others do to us? _____ We can still forgive others a lot easier when we remember how Jesus forgave us. Forgiveness does not mean the person does not deserve punishment. Jesus still took our punishment for sin. It just means He pardoned our iniquities. What a wonderful gift!

2. Colossians 2:13 says, "And you, being dead in your trespasses and the uncircumcision of your flesh, He has made alive together with Him, having forgiven you all trespasses."

Have you ever been around paramedics when someone has stopped breathing? That person is temporarily dead, but when the medical hero breathes life-giving air into the victim, he or she can start breathing again and become alive. It reminds me of what we were like before we were saved. Before you were changed by Jesus, you were actually spiritually dead because of the unredeemed and fallen desires coming from within your sin nature. But now you have been made alive in Christ because He has breathed His forgiveness into you!

How many trespasses (sins) has He forgiven you? _____Did you figure out the number? It is higher than we could count. When Jesus forgave your sins, it included ALL your sins. Does "all" ever mean "some"? _____ If Jesus had just forgiven your sins up until the time you prayed and asked forgiveness, would you still be forgiven forever? _____We can still choose to commit sins every day because we still live in our flesh, but God continues to clean us constantly until we get to heaven. Then we will receive perfect bodies. Are you glad He continues to forgive you for ALL of your sins? _____

3. The story of Joseph is in chapters 35 to 50 of Genesis. Read it when you have time. It is a very interesting story that will encourage you. For now, read **Genesis 45:5**. What did Joseph say to his brothers in verse five? _____

_____

_____

Even though Joseph's brothers had sold him as a slave, Joseph saw God's hand in the midst of his troubles. He did not blame his brothers for selling him as a slave. God had put Joseph in Egypt so he could save up grain before a famine came into the land. Joseph's troubles were used of God *to save many lives, including those of his family.* Joseph was able to forgive because he knew God's Word is true that says, "And we know that all things work together for good to those who love God, to those who are the called according to His purpose" (Romans 8:28). You can have the strength to forgive others as Joseph did when you know that Jesus has forgiven you when you did not deserve it. You can also know that if you look for the good in any situation, God will reveal it to you and bring blessings from it. No matter how terribly you have been treated by others, your grief was not greater than the sin debt we owed our Lord! Jesus forgave you of the greatest bill of all, your transgressions.

God does not have any anger toward you or a desire to punish you. Your sin has already been punished by the only perfect Substitute: Jesus Christ. He covered your sin by paying for it with His blood. It was not a canceled debt without payment. It was just paid for by Someone who could pay for it: Jesus. When you admitted your need to be forgiven of your sin by the only perfect One who can forgive you, then you were forgiven. That is an awesome gift. Now you can say, "*I am forgiven!*"

Are you remembering to fill in all the blanks? If not, go back and make sure you fill in all the "I am" blanks.

DAY 2

More Gifts! Can it Get any Better?

Memorization: Think about the meaning as you recite the memorization five times.

1. <u>Ephesians 1:3</u> "Blessed be the God and Father of our Lord Jesus Christ, who has blessed us with every spiritual blessing in the heavenly places in Christ."

2. <u>1 John 5:4</u> "For whatever is born of God overcomes the world. And this is the victory that has overcome the world—our faith."

3. <u>Hebrews 13:5b and 6a</u> "I will never leave you nor forsake you. ...The LORD is my helper."

   <u>Books of the Bible</u>: (New Testament continued) Galatians, Ephesians, Philippians, Colossians, 1 and 2 Thessalonians, 1 and 2 Timothy, Titus…

Dear Lord Jesus, I praise Your holy name for all the blessings of my salvation. Please open my eyes to how You continually cleanse me of sin so I am guaranteed eternity as Your child. Show me how I can serve You more fully today and in the future. In Jesus' name, Amen.

- **I was Ungodly/Unclean**
  (Romans 5:6)

- **I am**_____.
  (1 Cor. 6:11; 2 Tim. 2:21; Rom. 15:16; Heb. 10:10-14)

Marriage Advice

At my wedding shower, my grandmother said to me with all seriousness, "Are you sure you want to get married? You will be doing dishes the rest of your life!" She was constantly washing dishes, so that was from her perspective. Why did she scrub plates and utensils so much? It was so we would not get sick, right? Would you eat food off a plate that had been cleaned only once a month or once a year? Of course not. This story reminds me of how thankful we are that God washes our "dishes" many times a day by constantly cleansing us from the dirtiness of our sin.

1. Read **Hebrews 10:10-12.** (Hold your finger here.) How long are you sanctified (*purified from your sins*) according to verses 10-12? _____ These verses tell us that we are sanctified (cleansed) "*once for all*" and "*forever*" because of what Jesus did. That would mean that when Jesus paid for your wrong deeds with the sacrifice of His body on the cross, He was not only paying for PAST sins, but also paying for your PRESENT and FUTURE transgressions as well! In verse 10, it tells us that we have <u>positional</u> sanctification. This means <u>we are made His child and set aside for God's service</u>. This happens at the moment we are saved. It is when our position is first changed from unclean to clean. God gave one

offering—the offering of His body on the cross. This offering was a perfect offering that paid for our evil doings forever and did not need to be given again every time a person broke God's laws. You have positional sanctification forever. Once you admitted you needed Jesus to forgive you and believed in the offering of His body with His blood, that took care of it all for your positional sanctification. Our new position as His child sets us aside now for God's service.

2. Read **Hebrews 10:14**. In your own words, write down what God's Word says in verse 14. _____

    _____

In verse 14, it tells us that our cleansing is happening presently (*"those who are being sanctified"*) and continuing to cleanse us. This verse reveals to us another kind of sanctification. It is called progressive sanctification when God makes you like Him. It also begins the moment of salvation, so after being saved, we are slowly being made into the moral, spiritual, and mental image of Christ throughout our lifetime. We are progressing forward with constant cleansing that will be finished only when we are in the presence of the Lord and receive our new, sanctified body.

But remember, God's once and for all and perfected forever sacrifice does not give you a license to do wrong. If you sin, you will suffer the consequences of it just as a child suffers the punishment of disobedience toward a parent. But victory is available to you now!

Truth:

a) As a child of God, you have the Holy Spirit's power inside you now. You can choose to obey the Lord or deny that power and disobey Him.

b) If you sin after salvation, it will not change your position (relationship) as God's child. (*Relationship* means you are related to God; you are His child regardless of your actions.)

c) But if you do wrong, it will break your fellowship with your Heavenly Father until you confess it to Him, repent, and turn away from it. (Broken *fellowship* means you are not getting along well or not on speaking terms; you are a disobedient child of God.)

3. Read **1 Corinthians 6:11**. What are three ways God makes us clean from our sin?
    a) _____ b)_____ c) _____

When a doctor prepares to operate on a patient, he always sterilizes his instruments as well as his hands. Everything is purified from the germs so they will not cause infection or death. God has sterilized us from our "sin germs" so we can be completely pure. He even shows us a three-step sterilization process in 1 Corinthians 6:11. First, He *washes* us fully (that is forgiveness). Secondly, we are *sanctified* or purified (like being sterilized). Thirdly, we are *justified* or declared innocent before Him. This is just as if we have never sinned. Sanctified (*hagiazo*) in the Greek, means "to make holy, purify, or consecrate." We are going to go behind the scenes now and find out HOW God sanctifies us or makes us completely pure from our evil thoughts and deeds.

4. Who or what makes this happen? The following verses will take us on the trip to God's sterilization plant. John 17:17 says, "Sanctify them through Your truth: Your word is truth." What are we sanctified through? _____ Name two ways we are sanctified according to these next two verses. Read **Acts 26:18** and **Romans 15:16.** _____

_____

John 17:17 and 19 tells us we are sanctified through the *Word of God* which is the *truth*. Jesus, the Word, cleanses us as we read, study, and believe it. Acts 26:18 tells us we are sanctified by *faith*. Faith is our response to God's gift. When we accept forgiveness, it is by faith, by believing what Jesus, God's Son, has done on the cross for our fallen nature. Faith means that we do not see the cleansing with our physical eyes, but we see it with our spiritual eyes. The result is peace and joy through His forgiveness. We are declared innocent by justification and are ready to be used by God through sanctification. Romans 15:16 shows us we are sanctified (set apart) by the *Holy Ghost*, that is God Himself continually living in us and constantly cleansing us!

Now we know <u>HOW</u> we are sanctified. But <u>WHY</u> are we set apart for God's service? We already know God loves us and that we are owned by Him as His children and that He wants us to be with Him in heaven someday.

5. What is God's greater purpose in cleansing you from sin? 2 Timothy 2:21 says, "Therefore, if anyone cleanses himself from the latter, he will be a vessel for honor, sanctified and useful for the Master, prepared for every good work." _____

_____

_____

When a doctor sterilizes instruments to be used in an operation, it is for the purpose of using those instruments for something important, right? _____ Or does he disinfect them in order to just say they are his instruments and carry around in his bag because he is a doctor? _____ They are used to help make someone well who is sick or to even save a life. God, your spiritual Physician, decontaminated your sins in order to use you for something great! God has made you clean through the holy Word of God. You are also made pure because of your faith in what Jesus did on the cross for you. Now you are continually made innocent because God has given Himself in the form of the Holy Spirit to live inside of you. It is like having a sterilizing machine attached to your blood that cleanses you in every moment. That is why you can be sanctified forever and be accepted as God's child! According to 2 Timothy 2:21, because we are sanctified, we are *ready to be used by the master (Jesus) as one who honors Him because we are cleansed and prepared to do good works for God.*

As we obey God's purpose for us, we will be a blessing to others and ultimately have a part in being used by God in at least two major ways:

a) <u>Tell others the Good News (Gospel) of Jesus Christ</u>. When other people are saved, we can have a part in seeing their lives saved from eternal death! This is called witnessing or being a soul winner.

b) <u>Help others grow stronger in their faith</u> and reach God's purpose for their lives. This is called discipling others.

You were not saved just to go to heaven. You have a greater purpose to accomplish while on earth. It is called <u>progressive</u> sanctification, which is God making you like Him. This happens slowly over your lifetime, making you into the moral, spiritual, and mental image of Christ. This is forming your testimony so others will see Jesus in you and want to be saved too. They will see your changed life shining the attitudes and actions of Jesus more and more, and you can share with them how to become God's child. Because of being sanctified (spiritually sterilized by position), you are ready for God, the Great Physician, to use you as His special assistant to do the good work of helping others become sanitized from their sin germs when you lead them to Jesus. As you serve God in your church in a variety of ways, you are having a part in all who come to Jesus through the ministry of your church! As you study God's Word more and more, you will learn how to talk to people on your own about how to accept Jesus in their lives and become forgiven of all their sins too. Remember that you are positionally sanctified forever and being progressively sanctified constantly. Now you can say, *"I am sanctified!"*

DAY 3
I am Very Special

Memorization: Play the erase game today with one verse. Say others five times.

1. **Ephesians 1:3** "Blessed be the God and Father of our Lord Jesus Christ, who has blessed us with every spiritual blessing in the heavenly places in Christ."

2. **1 John 5:4** "For whatever is born of God overcomes the world. And this is the victory that has overcome the world—our faith."

3. **Hebrews 13:5b and 6a** "I will never leave you nor forsake you. …The LORD is my helper."

   Books of the Bible: (New Testament continued) Galatians, Ephesians, Philippians, Colossians, 1 and 2 Thessalonians, 1 and 2 Timothy, Titus…

Father God, may You be praised for Your purity, yet You love me unconditionally. Cleanse me of any impurity today and soften my heart to be more submissive to You and understand what You want me to apply to my life today from Your Word. Help me to learn to be as committed to You as You are to me. In Jesus' name, Amen.

- **I was Married to the World.**
  (1 John 2:15)

- **I am the** _____.
  (Isaiah 62:5; 2 Corinthians 11:2; Revelation 19:7)

1. According to **1 John 2:15**, when you loved the world, what was not yet in you?_____
   _____You did not have the *love of the Father* until you accepted it from Him.

2. Read **2 Corinthians 6:14-18.** What does God tell you not to do? (vs. 14 and 17)
   _____

What are two reasons why it does not work well for unbelievers and believers to date, be marriage partners, best friends, roommates, or even business partners? _____
_____
_____

Now that you are God's bride, He expects you to be loyal to Him. God says *not to be unequally yoked* or connected *together with unbelievers*. It makes sense that a *righteous person* (because of God in you) *does not think the same* or enjoy the same lifestyle *as a person who is in lawlessness (sin). A believer (one with God's light inside) will not enjoy spending time with a non-believer (one who is in the darkness of sin).* This means you are changed and are in a new family. You will have different beliefs, desires, and behavior. You should <u>not spend a lot of time</u> around the ungodly because their lifestyles are contrary to what God's Word teaches us. But you <u>should still spend a little time</u> with the unsaved so you can show them the love of Christ, pray for them, and tell them how to be forgiven and choose the Lord (Matthew 28:19; Acts 1:8, 13:47, 26:18; Romans 10:14-15). They need to see your changed life! But their sinful ways can rub off on you and pull you down, so you need to be careful about the amount of time you spend with unbelievers or even disobedient believers. Your enemy, Satan, will try to use unbelievers and disobedient believers to trick you into disobeying God. Realize you are human and can fall in your own strength. It is too easy to become like those whom you are around a lot. If a good apple is close to a rotten apple, does it influence the good apple to become better? _____The rotten apple will change the good apple into rotten fruit if the two stay together long enough. An obedient believer will not allow himself to be influenced by non-believers. (Exodus 23:2; 1 Corinthians 15:33; Proverbs 13:20; and Ephesians 5:8 and 11.)

3. Spiritually speaking, all believers are called the Bride of Christ. We must keep ourselves pure from the world and be faithful to Him. Read **Isaiah 62:5** and **2 Corinthians 11:2.** What two ways does God show you He loves you as His bride? _____ _____ He is totally in love and shows you by *rejoicing* over you. He also has a *Godly jealousy* for you if you wander away from Him and are not faithful to Him.

4. Read **Revelation 19:7.** How do you think we are to act as the "bride to be" of Christ? _____ _____ We are to be in love with Christ and be a *joyful* Christian, one who enjoys being with Christ, our Bridegroom, and *honor* Him. The Marriage of the Lamb will be the supper He has prepared for us as soon as we get to heaven. This is like a reception, and God is rejoicing over you as His bride. *We are to make ourselves ready for His return.* How? It is by living a pure life, obeying His commands, loving Him by spending time with Him, being faithful to God, and not loving another person or thing more than God. We are also to give Him praise and glory by serving Him and telling others how they can know Him as we do. A marriage to Christ is not like an earthly marriage. Each believer, man or woman, is already spiritually one with Christ. It simply means you are like God's own spouse—loyal, faithful, and in love with your Lord Jesus Christ—the perfect Bridegroom. Now you can say, *"I am the bride of Christ!"*

- **My Life was Like a House Built on Sand.** (Matthew 7:26-27)
- **I am the _____ of God and I am Building my Life on the _____.** (1 Corinthians 3:16; 6:15-20; Psalm 28:1; Matthew 7:24-25, 21:12)

1. Have you ever been to the beach and spent hours building a beautiful sand castle? What happens to it after a few hours? _____ Why do we spend time building something that will be destroyed so quickly? There is no harm in building a sand castle and it falling down because it is just for fun. Read **Matthew 7:24-27.**

What harm can come from building your life on the sand—any foundation other than the Word of Jesus Christ (vs. 27)? _____ Do you know anyone ignorant enough to build a real house on the sand? That act would be very foolish. The house would have a lot of destruction and *fall* as soon as the first rain came, if not before the person could even build the frame. What does God say about the characteristics of a wise man in verses 24-25? _____ The wise man *hears* (listens to God's Word) *and obeys* Him, whereas the foolish man hears the same instruction and does not obey God. What happens to the house built on the rock when the storm came? _____ Do you want to fall and be destroyed or stand and win? _____ If you are wise, you will not only hear the truth of God's Word, but you will obey it! This is building your life on the Rock, Jesus Christ. He is your sure foundation and will never fail you. You are not building a life of no importance.

2. Read **1 Corinthians 3:16.** How has your body changed since becoming saved? _____ _____ You are so special and important to God that He has chosen you to be *His temple*, His dwelling place. A temple or church must be kept clean. We must respect God's house. We also need to respect our body, which is God's house.

3. Read **1 Corinthians 6:15-20 and Hebrews 13:4.** Just as a bride is to keep herself pure for her husband, you are to keep your body temple pure for God. In marriage, two become one flesh. In the spiritual marriage to God, we actually become one with God. What is one sin (*vs. 18*) that causes us to sin against God and our own body? _____ When the Holy Spirit lives inside you, you need to respect Him enough to not take Him into places of evil and not allow your body (also His home) to participate in *sexual immorality*. This includes any sex outside of marriage (man and woman) as in (premarital sex, or living together as husband and wife without being lawfully married, or to be unfaithful to your husband or wife, or even same sex immorality). Anything you choose to do that would bring disease to your body, spiritually or physically, is also hurting the temple of God. We need to take only spiritually and physically healthy things into our mouths, eyes, nose, and ears. Why do you need to be this careful with your body (see vs. 20)? _____ _____

If you buy an item, you can decide what to do with it and how to treat it, right? *God bought you for a very expensive price—His blood, His life* (Ephesians 1:7). He owns you! You are to show Him how grateful you are and others how wonderful He is by the way you live your life. You agreed to accept His free gift; therefore, you owe Him. You will never be able to pay Him back! But your loyalty in respecting the temple He made and dwells in is the least you can do. God tells us all to respect our temple also because it protects us from a lot of heartache and disease.

4. Read **2 Corinthians 5:10.** What will happen to all believers one day? _____ All Christians will stand before Christ and be *judged* for what we did in our body, whether it was good or bad. This is not to determine if we were saved. That was already decided and cannot be taken away if it was a real salvation change. This judgment is to hand out rewards for the good works we have done for the Lord. But we do not want to be embarrassed for the

disobedient acts we did in our body, do we? _____ He wants you to be clean of sin because you are His temple. God is holy, and He cannot be defiled. As a Christian, if you have defiled your body, you can start today fresh and clean! Repent and remember how special your body is in God's eyes. You are so special that He chose to dwell in you! Take care of His house. Now you can say with joy because you love Jesus and He loves you, "*I am the Temple of God, and I am building my life on the Rock of Jesus Christ!*"

DAY 4
Closer than Family

Memorization: Play the erase game today with another verse. Say others five times.

1. **Ephesians 1:3** "Blessed be the God and Father of our Lord Jesus Christ, who has blessed us with every spiritual blessing in the heavenly places in Christ."

2. **1 John 5:4** "For whatever is born of God overcomes the world. And this is the victory that has overcome the world—our faith."

3. **Hebrews 13:5b and 6a** "I will never leave you nor forsake you. ...The LORD is my helper."

   Books of the Bible: (New Testament continued) Galatians, Ephesians, Philippians, Colossians, 1 and 2 Thessalonians, 1 and 2 Timothy, Titus...

Father God, thank You for being my perfect Father and showing me what it means to be part of the family of God forever. Open my eyes to how my sin is fully paid for and the wonderful inheritance You have provided for me. Show me how to apply these truths to my daily life so I can please You in all areas. In Jesus' name, Amen.

A School for Animals

As a child, did you ever watch a bird build a nest and wonder if there was a school for birds that taught them how to do that? Or did you watch bees in a hive and wonder how they know how to organize their workforce to accomplish the task of making honey? Ants are another army of creatures who seem to know what they are doing. None of these creatures had bird, bee, or ant classes; they just naturally know what to do. It is called instinct and is necessary for their survival. There is another kind of nature we humans have, but instead of it helping us survive, it hinders our life in many ways. It is called the sin nature. We naturally know how to do wrong. No one taught us how to hit, disobey, steal, cheat, talk ugly, fight, or be selfish. How did we get like that? Find out by reading the verses below.

- **I was of Adam—having a Sin Nature.** (Romans 5:12, 19, 7:14-25; Psalm 51:3, 5)
- **I am of _____, in His _____.** (1 Corinthians 12:27, 15:22; Romans 12:4-5)

1. Did you ever wonder what caused evil and suffering to come into the world? This is the answer. Romans 5:12 and 19 says, "Therefore, just as through one man sin entered the world, and death through sin, and thus death spread to all men, because all sinned. For as by one man's disobedience many were made sinners, so also by one Man's obedience many will be made

righteous." Adam passed the "sin disease" on to you and me when he and Eve committed the first sin. What else spread to all people? _____ We have the curse of being sinners and *will also die* someday too. We all inherited this awful disease. But how are we cured of this evil illness (see vs. 19)? _____ The All God /All Man—*Jesus Christ* became obedient to God and paid for your sin on the cross and rose again. As soon as you accept this gift payment, you are removed from the curse of sin and death spiritually. You can live forever in heaven and not die in your sin. Then you are considered righteous, or in right standing with God because of Jesus. Instead of being from your father Adam, who passed the sin nature to you, you switch fathers and families and become *of God!*

2. Read **1 Corinthians 12:27.** Verse 27 says we are part of the _____ _____. This means that believers are not only a temple of God, but also part of His larger family, the body of believers in the church too. You are part of the *body of Christ.* When you have a hurt toe, something in your eye, or a burned finger, do you ignore it or take care of it? _____ Just as every member of your physical body is important, so each person who is a member of the body of Christ is important. Each one needs love and encouragement and help at times. If you love Jesus, you will love His body, His family (other Christians) and help them when they are hurting or in need. The brothers and sisters you have in the same family with God can sometimes be closer than your physical family. Jesus said in Matthew 25:40b, "Inasmuch as you did it to one of the least of these My brethren, you did it unto Me." When you treat others with love, God says it is the same as showing love to Him. When you treat others in an unloving way, you are treating God the same way. He loves His own children just as parents love their children and just as you love your own body. What a wonderful blessing to know that God is not only your Father, but you are part of His body of believers! Now you can say, "*I am of God, in His body*! I am His family!"

- **I was Owned by the Devil.**   • **I am** _____.
   (John 8:44)   (1 Peter 1:18-19; Ephesians 1:7; 1 Corinthians 6:20)

1. Do you have any troublemakers or outcasts in your family? We all know someone who has caused trouble or heartache. We may have caused it at one time or another. Who was the first to cause trouble in our original family? It was our ancestor Adam, who passed the curse of sin down to all mankind. But where did Adam get this curse? Look at **John 8:44.** Who became Adam's father because of his disobedience to God? _____ All mankind, including you and me, started out with the *devil* as our father. The devil is the first troublemaker. Praise God, he is not your father anymore once you were saved!

1 Peter 1:18-19 says, "Knowing that you were not redeemed with corruptible things, like silver or gold, from your aimless conduct received by tradition from your fathers, but with the precious blood of Christ, as of a lamb without blemish and without spot."

2. Ephesians 1:7 says, "In Him we have redemption through His blood, the forgiveness of sins, according to the riches of His grace." No one would be able to redeem (pay a ransom) your sin with money or things that can fade away. What is the only way you can be redeemed

(ransomed or paid in full)? _____ One of the names of Jesus is "Lamb of God." He told the Israelites to sacrifice a lamb (one without any spot or blemish) by killing it on an altar. They were to ask for forgiveness of their sins this way as they looked forward to the time that the Messiah would be the substitute, the real Lamb of God that would be sacrificed on the cross for their wrong deeds. They looked to the future when the Messiah would be the sacrifice, but we now look to the past when the Messiah gave His life for our sins. But His sacrifice covered all sins in the past, present, and future for those who accept it by faith. Once Jesus came to die and pay for our sins with His perfect blood, the lamb sacrifice was no longer needed. After Christ's resurrection from the dead, Christians and Jews and anyone else must ask forgiveness for their sins by believing in Jesus Christ as the Lamb of God. The only way we are all redeemed is *through His precious blood*. Christ paid the ransom. He paid it all! Now you can say, "*I am redeemed!*"

- **I was a Servant of Sin.**
  (Ecclesiastes 7:20; Romans 7:14)

- **I am a** _____.
  (Revelation 15:3)

Have you ever known anyone who was a servant of a rich person? Does this person do whatever he or she wants or does he or she have to obey the master? _____ As a result of being born in sin (Psalm 51:5), we did not have a choice to choose right, only wrong because we were of our father Satan (John 8:44). Because we were born with the sin disease, we had wicked desires and did wrong deeds. Sin started with the devil, whom God calls the "father of lies." Then mankind chose to sin (after being tempted by the Evil One), and sin was passed on to you and me. But when you became a Christian, you were not powerless anymore. You were adopted by a new Master, the Lord Jesus Christ! Now you have power from your Heavenly Father to be an overcomer! Does that mean you are a saint too? Let's find out.

Have you heard of Mother Teresa or others who have done a lot of good deeds for mankind? These people are called "saints" in our world. Are they real saints? Does doing good deeds make a person a saint according to God? Let's see what He says. 2 Thessalonians 1:10 says, "When He comes, in that Day, to be glorified in His saints and to be admired among all those who believe, because our testimony among you was believed." The saints are described as those who _____. Saints are not people we know on earth who seem to have exceptional holiness or abilities. All *believers*, counting you, are saints according to God. He has sanctified you, and that makes you a saint!

Since all people who are saved are saints, how does that determine how we should live? Fill in the blanks to 2 Thessalonians 1:10 to find the answer.

"When He comes, in that Day, to be _____ in His saints and to be _____ among all those who believe, because our _____ among you was believed" (2 Thessalonians 1:10.)

We are to *glorify* God by our obedience to His Word and love for others. Then God will be *admired* by other believers. Why will this happen? It will happen only if our *testimony* reflects Jesus Christ's attitudes, actions, and words. Then others will believe Jesus is real and that we are true Christians! Our life will draw them to be saved and develop a growing relationship with Christ. So as a saint of God, are we to live to make ourselves look good, or to make Jesus look good? _____

Read **Acts 26:18**. What did you receive because you are a sanctified saint of God? _____
_____

When you were *forgiven*, you received an *inheritance* as a saint of God. God has already given us so much as His children. Let's make Jesus look good! Now you can say, "*I am a saint who serves my Lord Jesus Christ!*"

Let's review who you are now!

IX. Who I Am Now – Before and After Pictures

    A. I am a New Creature.
    B. I am Born Again and Complete in Christ.
    C. I am Saved and Guaranteed Eternity.
    D. I am now God's Friend.
    E. I am Loved Unconditionally Forever.
    F. I am a Child of God, Adopted by Him as my Heavenly Father.
    G. I am Royalty. The King of kings is my Father.
    H. I am a Chosen Generation, a Royal Priest, a Holy Nation, a Special People.
    I. I am Justified.
    J. I am Forgiven.
    K. I am Sanctified.
    L. I am the Bride of Christ.
    M. I am the Temple of God, and I am Building my Life on the Rock of Jesus Christ.
    N. I am of God, in His Body.
    O. I am Redeemed.
    P. I am a Saint that Serves my Lord Jesus Christ.

Look how God has changed you! This is just the beginning. Let's find out more about what you have because of Christ.

Thank You, Lord Jesus, for changing me in so many ways to honor You. Please help me to remember these truths about who I am now and live with a victorious attitude. In Jesus' name, Amen.

DAY 5

It's Time to Open My Birthday Presents

Memorization: Say the verses five times and you almost have them memorized!

1. **Ephesians 1:3** "Blessed be the God and Father of our Lord Jesus Christ, who has blessed us with every spiritual blessing in the heavenly places in Christ."

2. **1 John 5:4** "For whatever is born of God overcomes the world. And this is the victory that has overcome the world—our faith."

3. **Hebrews 13:5b and 6a** "I will never leave you nor forsake you. …The LORD is my helper."

   Books of the Bible: (New Testament continued) Galatians, Ephesians, Philippians, Colossians, 1 and 2 Thessalonians, 1 and 2 Timothy, Titus…

Lord Jesus, thank You for making everything new at my birth into Your family. Please make my heart clean and ready to understand and apply the truths in the Scriptures today. Cause my heart to rejoice in the abundance of blessings that are mine because of Your gift of eternal life. In Jesus' name, Amen.

God's Gifts That Tell What I Have in Christ

Remember this important fact: who you are in Christ NEVER CHANGES! Just as you cannot change the blood in your body that proves you are from certain parents, so you cannot change the fact that God is your Father once you are His child. Now that you know a lot more of who you are in Christ, what do you have in Christ because of your new status?

When our first child was born, we had so much fun planning her first birthday party. We hosted it at a beautiful park by a lake. All our friends showed up with all kinds of wonderful gifts for her. We even had a missionary friend who gave her a unique purse from Africa. It was so special. When you were born, your parents or caregivers prepared many gifts to give you. God, your Heavenly Father, has given you spectacular presents, too. They are so much more valuable than anything given to you at your birthday parties! Now that you are in His family, salvation is only the beginning of the gifts He has given you. What are other presents from your Heavenly Father? Read on and get a glimpse of what God has given you now. Look up the following verses and answer the questions to find out some exciting surprises!

Because I have Believed by Faith in Jesus Christ:

- I have a _____.

Read **2 Peter 1:4.** What have you escaped? _____

What have you been given? _____
As God's child, you have escaped the *corruption* in the world *through lust* or evil desires. This means you have escaped the power that sin has over you, and you will not perish in hell for eternity. What good news! And you have been given many *precious promises* as well as a new, *divine nature.* "Divine" means it is from God. Your inward man has changed because you now have God's desires living in you (2 Cor. 5:17). You have a new nature and a deep desire to go the right way. You will feel sad, guilty, and uncomfortable if you sin. You will want to please God now. You will be joyful when you obey the principles in God's Word because that is in line with God's Holy Spirit living inside you. But if you are really saved, you will be miserable if you stray from God, that is, disobey Him.

Read **Romans 7:18-25.** Do you ever feel like you have a war going on inside you? On one hand, you want to obey God. But on the other hand, you struggle with some bad habits or sins and do wrong sometimes. Cheer up. You have the power inside you to have victory more often! How do you have victory? See verses 22 and 25. _____
_____

You can choose to give in to the temptation to sin, which is the natural tendency you have because you still live in your body and are in the world. But if you want to win more victories, you need to get away from the people, places, or other things that tempt you. Then you can choose *to delight in God's law (His Word)* and *with your mind decide to serve Christ.* How is this possible? The more you are in the Bible

> You will be joyful when you obey God's principles in His Word... You will be miserable if you go away from God, that is, disobey Him.

daily and attend church and Bible studies, the more your mind will grow to think like the mind of God. This is like you are feeding your mind the proper spiritual nutrients. Then you will begin to gain victory over sin in your life and experience more joy! Will you let sin control you or God? _____ It is your choice and your chance to show God you love Him and are grateful for all the gifts He has given you. You received the new nature when you were born into God's family. Because of this, you have God's strength in you now, helping you obey Him. You do not have to keep surrendering to the temptations in the flesh. Be brave and run from them. You can start experiencing the abundant life God has planned for you. You can say *"I have a new nature!"* Let's find out more about God's plan for you.

- I have a _____.

Read **Galatians 4:6.** How do you know you are a son or daughter of God? Who has been sent to live in your heart to make it possible? _____
The Holy Spirit is the same as God's Spirit, the *Spirit of His Son.* (You should see a capital "S"

in front of Spirit when the Bible is talking about the Holy Spirit and a lowercase "s" when it is talking about man's spirit.) God says, "And if Christ is in you, the body is dead because of sin, but the Spirit is life because of righteousness. But if the Spirit of Him who raised Jesus from the dead dwells in you, He who raised Christ from the dead will also give life to your mortal bodies through His Spirit who dwells in you" (Romans 8:10-11). Is this exciting? _____ Your spirit has also been reborn. You have a new Spirit. You were dead spiritually, but now you are alive forever! Romans 8:16 says, "The Spirit Himself bears witness with our spirit that we are children of God." Now you can say "*I have a new Spirit!*"

- I have a _____.

Read **Isaiah 61:10**. What has God clothed you with? _____
When a poor child is adopted from another country, that child receives new clothing. This gift shows that the child has new parents. Once saved, we are God's children, so our new status must have new *garments of salvation* and a *robe of righteousness*. Revelation 6:11a says, "Then a white robe was given to each of them." Not only did you receive a new nature and a new Spirit, you received new garments. Your white robe of righteousness was given to you because you repented of your sin and Jesus changed you with His blood. You have been made clean. Do you put on clean clothes after taking a bath or put on dirty clothes? _____ When God turned you around, you began to go a different direction! Wearing new spiritual clothing shows you are clean like Jesus and are allowed entrance into God's kingdom. It is also a picture of the purity of being a bride of Christ. Now you can say "I have a *white robe of righteousness* for my new clothing!"

- I have _____.

Read **Matthew 25:34.** We know some friends who inherited a mansion with lots of land, a pool, a pond, horses, a tennis court, and a life not having to worry about money. Maybe that is nice on earth, but you and I have it even better. We have inherited the kingdom of God in heaven forever and ever, and no one can take it away! His gift of eternal life starts the moment you prayed to receive Jesus as your personal Savior. The inheritance of eternal life in heaven also means that you are an heir of God and will reign with the King of kings someday. Now you can say "*I have an inheritance that will be mine forever!*"

- I have _____ to God!

Read **1 John 5:14-15.** If you were given the keys to a president's home or a king's palace, you would be able to access it at any time. Would you feel privileged? _____ God has given you the keys to access Him at any time. You are able to pray to God at any time and in any place. You are His privileged, royal child. Ephesians 3:12 says, "In whom we have boldness and access with confidence through faith in Him." You can be bold and talk to your Father-King because you can say "I have *access to God* at any time and in any place!" Is it awesome to be so loved and privileged? _____ Find out about more gifts tomorrow when we continue to open them. Did you fill out all the blanks with the answers of your presents from God?

DAY 6
Abundant Gifts Galore

<u>Memorization:</u> Say it five times. Then say them to a friend or family member.

1. <u>**Ephesians 1:3**</u> "Blessed be the God and Father of our Lord Jesus Christ, who has blessed us with every spiritual blessing in the heavenly places in Christ."

2. <u>**1 John 5:4**</u> "For whatever is born of God overcomes the world. And this is the victory that has overcome the world—our faith."

3. <u>**Hebrews 13:5b and 6a**</u> "I will never leave you nor forsake you. ...The LORD is my helper."

   <u>**Books of the Bible**</u>: (New Testament continued) Galatians, Ephesians, Philippians, Colossians, 1 and 2 Thessalonians, 1 and 2 Timothy, Titus…

_____

Lord Jesus, thank You for being so good to me. Cleanse me and open my eyes to what You would have me apply from Your Word today. Help me to bask in the joy of knowing You even more than the abundant blessings You have given me at salvation. In Jesus' name, Amen.

More Gifts Coming Up! Following are many gifts that are overflowing continually to you as you need them throughout your life. It is like they are "time-released." They are all ABUNDANT gifts.

• Read **Numbers 14:18a. I have been given abundant _____.**

This means you are spared from punishment you deserve. Mercy describes God's attitude toward you as one in distress. You were given mercy at salvation, and He continues to give it to you in any day-to-day situation that you need it. That is *abundant mercy!*

• Read **Ephesians 2:7. I have abundant _____.**

Favor (or love) you did not deserve is called grace. Have you ever felt sorry for a child being punished and told him or her you would give him or her grace this time? God was able to give you grace only because your sin was paid for. Having abundant *grace* is a huge relief when you were guilty, right? _____

• Read **John 10:10.** It tells you why Jesus came.

You can say: **I have _____ more abundantly now!**

We will experience our abundant life when we obey God's commands. He tells us how to have true joy in any circumstance. The Christian life, when lived as God intended, is the most joyful life you could ever have! It is an abundant *life*.

- Read **Ephesians 3:20. I have** _____ **from God!**

As long as we are asking in God's will and with the power of faith in God, this verse says that there is no limit to what God can do in your life. He wants to give you more than you could imagine or dream up! How do you allow God's blessing to be on your life in this way?

What does verse twenty say? It is "according to what"? _____

We must release the *power that works in us*—God's power with our faith. Just like a stick of dynamite has the power to blow up whatever is around it, it will not work unless it is ignited.

You can say, "I have *abundant power from God!*"

- Read **Philippians. 4:19. God gives you an abundant** _____.

He promises to take care of you in every situation. Think of a time when God came through to supply something you needed. Was it a bill that needed to be paid, or food, or clothes? Was it an emotional need? Did He send you words of encouragement through a friend? Write a time God supplied your need: _____

The Lord provides for you many times every day. All Christians can say, "I have an abundant *supply from God!*" I never have to worry. Luke 12:6-7 tells us how much God cares for the birds. If God cares for the birds, He cares for you more.

- Read **Psalm 91:11 and Hebrews 1:14.**
  I have _____ _____ **to protect me.**

You have your own army of bodyguards, and they are invisible. Sometimes they do their work silently and you never even realize they have protected you. Other times it may be more obvious.

The Unusual Bike Ride

When my daughter was learning how to ride a bike, we decided to go practice without training wheels by riding down our street. As she was putting on her helmet, I heard in my thoughts a small, still voice saying, "Make sure you make her helmet tight. It could save her life someday." I realized it was God who had warned me so her life could be saved! I knew that something was about to happen, and I became afraid. I almost decided not to let her ride her bike that day. But then I felt the Lord was saying that if I did not trust Him when I had been warned, then there may be another time I would not be notified. This was my one chance to trust God in this situation. I did not want to be unprepared later. I did not tell my daughter this had happened. This was unusual and not something that had happened before. So I asked God to protect her as I made sure her helmet was as tight as possible. I told God that I trusted Him with her life, and I needed Him to come through. I decided I would run along with her and try to prevent any wreck that could hurt her, but that was humanly impossible. When she arrived at the end of the street, just barely out of my reach, she wrecked very quickly. Her helmet hit the street curb with such force that it knocked it off her head. I nervously checked her, and she was fine. God came through, of course. Her head and body were not hurt. Praise the Lord! If that helmet had not been on tight when that happened, it would have shifted and not protected her head. I know it would have killed her because of the warning I received. But God sent His guardian angels. Now you can also say, "I have *guardian angels* to protect me all the time!"

- Read **2 Corinthians 6:18** and **Hebrews 13:5b.**
  I have a _____ who will never _____ me.

What does God say He will never do? _____ You are His what? _____ Are you glad God keeps His promise of *never leaving you* alone? He is your Faithful Father, and you are His *son or daughter*. He always plans for your good. Now you can say, "I have a *Father* who will never *leave* me!"

- Read **1 Corinthians 10:13** and **15:57.**
  I have _____ over sin and troubles because of the _____ God has given me!

What will God do to help you out when you are tempted to sin? _____ He will *provide a way out* because He gives you the power to resist the devil and obey God. But it is your choice. What is it that helps you overcome the temptations in the world? _____ If you desire to have victory over sin and problems, it is essential that you become strengthened through time with Jesus in His Word and prayer. This will give you more *faith* in God and His promises. 1 John 5:4 says, "For whatever is born of God overcomes the world. And this is the victory that has overcome the world—our faith." You can now say, "I have *victory* over sin and troubles because of the *faith* God has given me!"

- Read **John 14:27. I have _____ from God that passes all understanding!**

What does this verse tell us that God gives you? _____
How do you keep it? _____
Do not choose to let your heart *be troubled* (worried) or *afraid*. If you fear instead of believing and having faith, then you will not use the gift of peace that God has given you. When children are afraid, they can be taught to 1.) Pray to Jesus about it. 2.) Quote a verse that they know out loud. 3.) Read verses from the Bible until they feel God's peace. So can we! Now you can say, "I have *peace* from God that passes all understanding!"

- Read **1 Peter 4:11. I have new _____ to serve my Father and Lord!**

You have many more abilities that you received when you became God's child. They are called spiritual gifts of service. You found out what spiritual gifts you possess when you filled out the Spiritual Gifts Profile in Appendix H. You will learn more about these in the next book, *Part 2: Walking in the Light*. We have no excuse for not serving God. These gifts will glorify God, that is, allow others to see how awesome He is. Now you can say, "I have new *abilities* to serve my Father and Lord!" Think about the value of these gifts. Even one is worth more than gold. God loves you so much. These gifts are only the beginning. Take time now to thank God for all the blessings He has already given you!

Let's review some blessings of what you have in Christ now!

X. God's Gifts That Tell What You Have in Christ

<u>Because I have Believed by Faith in Jesus Christ</u>:

  A. I Have a New Nature.
  B. I Have a New Spirit.
  C. I Have a White Robe of Righteousness for My New Clothing.
  D. I Have an Inheritance that will be Mine Forever.
  E. I Have Access to God.
  F. I Have been Given Abundant Mercy.
  G. I Have Abundant Grace.
  H. I Have Life More Abundantly Now.
  I. I Have Abundant Power from God.
  J. I Have an Abundant Supply from God.
  K. I Have Guardian Angels to Protect Me.
  L. I Have a Father Who will Never Leave Me.
  M. I Have Victory over Sin and Troubles Because of the Faith God has Given Me.
  N. I Have Peace from God that Passes All Understanding.
  O. I Have New Abilities to Serve My Father and Lord.

Write down a couple of your most favorite blessings God has given you from the above list:

_____

_____

Thank You, Lord Jesus, for giving me so much more than I could have imagined! These blessings are worth more than tons of gold. Thank You for being so good to me. Help me to live joyfully in these truths and praise Your name more often. In Jesus' name, Amen.

CHAPTER 5
God's Wonderful Purpose and Plan for My Life

DAY 1

The Right Architect

Memorization and Testimony: Say memory verses and books of the Bible five times.

1. **Jeremiah 29:11** "For I know the thoughts that I think toward you, says the LORD, thoughts of peace and not of evil, to give you a future and a hope."

2. **Romans 12:1-2** "I beseech you therefore, brethren, by the mercies of God, that you present your bodies a living sacrifice, holy, acceptable to God, which is your reasonable service. And do not be conformed to this world, but be transformed by the renewing of your mind, that you may prove what is that good and acceptable and perfect will of God."

3. **Testimony** – Share your testimony with a friend or family member this week.

   Books of the Bible: Review reciting Matthew through 1 and 2 Timothy. Now say: Titus, Philemon, Hebrews, James, 1st and 2nd Peter, 1st and 2nd and 3rd John, Jude, and Revelation.

Dear God, thank You that You are all-knowing and that I can trust You to guide me to make the right decisions in every area. Cleanse me and open my heart to hear from Your Word today and obey it. Help me to consult You first about any choices I may have each day. In Jesus' name, Amen.

The Right Architect

When I was little, I loved to draw house plans. It was so much fun to dream about what kind of house I wanted when I grew up. I drew the rooms in different places and different sizes. I would draw a wraparound porch or a tree growing out through the roof from the living room, or even a fountain with a pond. What would happen if someone had tried to build a house by using a child's house plans? _____

We all need to have a qualified architect design plans to build our dream house. It is the same way with God. He is the qualified architect in your life. He knows how to build your life according to His perfect and wonderful plan for you. Jeremiah 29:11 says, "For I know the thoughts that I think toward you, says the LORD, thoughts of peace and not of evil, to give you a future and a hope." Although this verse of Scripture directly applied to the nation of Israel, God was the same God then as He is today. Therefore, the principle we can gather from this verse is God still has a plan for you today!

God does not sit around thinking how He can bring troubles to you. His plans are always to bring about the best result and never to hurt you. He plans how you can have peace in your life. He wants to give you a future and a hope and has surprises waiting for you in your future (1 Corinthians 2:9; Jeremiah 29:11; Ephesians 3:20; James 1:17). His plans for you will build a life that will stand when storms come, and it will be beautiful and glorify Him. He is the perfect architect who knows what He is doing. When you and I try to design the plans for our life, we cannot be successful without God. We are like a little child dreaming of what we want and trying to make it happen without being qualified. Instead, we need to go to our Daddy God, Who knows so much more than we do. He sees the big picture and end result. He specifically designed your life to turn out better than you could imagine! This does not mean you will never have problems or sad situations. Life on this sin-cursed earth produces problems. It is not God's fault. But if you will keep trusting God, knowing that He is the Problem-Solver, and ask Him what you can learn through each situation, you will be able to go through anything with His strength. You can know that all areas of your life will turn out for good and successfully someday when you follow the blueprints made by your architect Father.

- **God Deserves All Honor, Glory, and Power**

Read **Revelation 4:11** and **5:12**. Why does God deserve to receive all honor, glory, and power?

_____

God created all things, including you. He is *the Lamb that was slain* for you! You were created because it was His will (desire) to create you. He is the Artist and can decide what to do with His creation. Does a professional artist have to listen to anyone as to how to make his creation? _____. When an artist creates a picture or any kind of artwork, he creates it from his mind and heart. Therefore, he can put his name on that artwork (Revelation 14:1 and Deuteronomy 28:10). God has put His name on you. You are His creation, and you exist for God's purposes, not for your own. It is all about God. It is not about you. The Creator gets to choose the purpose for the people He created. But God's purposes are perfect and are beneficial to you—better than you could plan or imagine. 1 Corinthians 2:9 says, "But as it is written: Eye has not seen, nor ear heard, nor have entered into the heart of man the things which God has prepared for those who love Him." What do you think this means? _____

_____

You *cannot even begin to imagine the wonderful plans God has for you,* especially for all those who love Him! Just as a little child imagines a dream home, God has a dream so much greater, and He can actually make it happen. Does this wonderful plan mean that everything will be perfect? No. But God can use the hard times in your life to bring about His wonderful plan. He will be with you and hold your hand and comfort you even when life gives you a bumpy road. He says in Romans 8:28, "And we know that all things work together for good to those who love God, to those who are the called according to His purpose." As you allow God to be in the driver's seat, the Boss in your life, then you will learn to trust in His expertise and not just your own knowledge. When you were young, you had to trust in your parents to drive the car and take you where you needed to go. What would have happened if you had gotten hold of the steering wheel? _____

Car Wash Disaster

One day, we were getting our car washed in a do-it-yourself car wash. Our children were little and were strapped in their car seats. All of a sudden, while I was rinsing the car, the car started moving. My husband saw the car rolling just in time and opened the door and put his foot on the brake just before our car almost crashed into a brick wall! Our toddler son had gotten hold of the steering wheel and shifted the car out of park and into drive. It could have wrecked our car and also hurt our children. This story reminds us of how easily we will wreck our lives unless we trust God to be in charge of the steering wheel of our lives. We are like a toddler compared to God's wisdom and knowledge. We have to let God direct us in the right direction in order to be safe and make it to the right place.

- **Ask God for Advice First**

Read **Proverbs 3:5 and 6.** In whom are you to trust? _____ What are you <u>not</u> to lean on? _____Who are you to ask first for advice, according to these verses? _____. When you trust (have faith) that the *LORD Jesus*, our Wonderful Counselor, will work out your situation, do not try to figure it out with *your* limited, human *understanding* and knowledge alone. Instead, pray and *ask God* what to do to work it out; He promises to show you which path to choose in your life. He will help you make the right daily decisions to steer you in the correct direction toward that wonderful plan and purpose He designed just for you. Going down the right path is the result of consulting God to help you make the right decisions. What are some decisions you have made in the past or still need to make in the future? Check all decisions that apply to you.

__ dating __ marriage __ career __ school __ children __ financial __ friends

__ church __ forgiveness __ moral decisions __ health decisions __ moving __ other

With all the decisions to make in life, we need a qualified, experienced guide that can tell us the best choices. Do you want to have a fulfilling life, one that will bring satisfaction and no regrets? _____ The Bible, written by God, is the handbook to read! Jesus, our Wonderful Counselor, is always available and never too busy. He has all wisdom from His Word for any decision you need to make.

DAY 2
The Secret of Success

Memorization: Say the memory verses and the books of the Bible five times.

1. <u>Jeremiah 29:11</u> "For I know the thoughts that I think toward you, says the LORD, thoughts of peace and not of evil, to give you a future and a hope."

2. <u>Romans 12:1-2</u> "I beseech you therefore, brethren, by the mercies of God, that you present your bodies a living sacrifice, holy, acceptable to God, which is your reasonable service. And do not be conformed to this world, but be transformed by the renewing of your mind, that you may prove what is that good and acceptable and perfect will of God."

3. <u>Testimony</u> – Share your testimony with a friend or family member this week.

   <u>**Books of the Bible**</u>: Review reciting Matthew through 1 and 2 Timothy. Now say Titus, Philemon, Hebrews, James, 1ˢᵗ and 2ⁿᵈ Peter, 1ˢᵗ and 2ⁿᵈ and 3ʳᵈ John, Jude, and Revelation.

Jesus, I love You. Thank You for being all-wise. Cause my heart to listen to Your Word today and obey You. Please show me how to seek Your wisdom and only listen to godly counsel so I can honor You with the right kind of success in my life. In Jesus' name, Amen.

- **Go to God's Success Manual**

1. What does God say in His Holy Book, the Word of God, about how to make successful decisions and the way to begin to gain knowledge? Read **Proverbs 1:7**. (Stay in Proverbs.) _____ _____What kind of person ignores wisdom and instruction? _____ If a person is willing to *fear the LORD*, he or she will have a holy reverence for Him by obeying His Word. But if someone is not willing to fear Him, God calls him a *"fool"* if he refuses to listen to Him. When we have a respect for God, we will realize how great and powerful He is and that He can punish us if we do not obey. We will also realize the rewards of obeying Him. God is the perfect parent, unlike the earthly parents we may have had. He disciplines us only in love in order to teach us to not go the wrong way. But He prefers that we listen to Him and go the right way so we can be rewarded with many blessings instead.

2. What are three characteristics of a wise person, one who has great understanding? Read **Proverbs 1:5.** *a)* _____ *b)*_____
   c) _____

This verse is a favorite because all answers in life can be solved if we just listen to God and to godly people He sends our way. Do you stop and *hear God* through His Word, to listen to Him or others long enough to learn from them? Do you work on *increasing your learning,* not only about God Himself, but in other subjects like health, rearing children, marriage, finances, and any other area that is important in making right decisions in life? _____ We need to *get advice from godly, wise counsel.* But many times, we are in a hurry and think we know all we need to know about an area. We brush over knowledge that could have helped us avoid trouble, gather more success, or even save a life of a friend!

3. Where is the best place to get wisdom, knowledge, and understanding? Check one:
    a. _____ Universities   b. _____ Educated People   c. _____ Family   d. _____ Good Books
    e. _____ Famous /Rich People   f. _____ The Bible   g. _____ TV/ Internet

Look at **Proverbs 2:6 and 3:6** for the answer. What is it? _____
_____

The best way to have wisdom is to *seek it from the LORD's mouth through God's Word and prayer.* You can still get advice from more education, books, and people, and you should; but be careful. Just because you get "education" does not mean it is the truth or the best choice. Human education changes depending on the time period and knowledge gathered at that time. But you will know the truth for all time when you spend much time reading and studying the Bible. God's Word never changes, is never out of date, but always appropriate for your current needs, problems, or decisions. Do not make decisions based only on your preconceived ideas and experience. You and I have limited knowledge and could be wrong. Always do thorough research to find out the truth in an area. Compare that advice to the wisest Author of all time—God. If the source disagrees with God's Word, then it will steer you in the wrong direction.

Jesus said in James 1:5, "If any of you lacks wisdom, let him ask of God, who gives to all liberally and without reproach, and it will be given to him." The previous verses (in James 1) were talking about trials (problems) that we go through in life. We will not become like Christ if we do not respond correctly to hardships. The first way of responding correctly is to *pray for wisdom* so we will know how to respond to every situation and allow God to develop His godly qualities in us. Most issues come from a wrong decision we have made. So asking God for wisdom will not only steer you in the right direction to solve your problem, but when you respond in wisdom, you will develop the character that is pleasing to God and will help fulfill His purpose in your life. Do not get in the habit of making a quick decision based on emotions. Do you want to go through difficulties many times because you did not learn the first time? _____ Be wise! Get into the habit of asking God for wisdom daily before you get in the middle of an emotional crisis. It is also wise to decide ahead of time how you will react to different situations and temptations as Daniel did. (See Daniel 1 for more study).

A Prayer to Protect and Guide You

Pray a prayer like this in Jesus' name now, and believe it.

Dear Jesus: Please help me get in the habit of listening to wise, godly counsel from the people who study and obey Your Word consistently. Open my eyes to recognize godly people You send my way and recognize those who are giving me wrong advice. Guide me to listen to Your Word above all others and understand its applications for me.

In Jesus' name, Amen.

Keep praying this kind of prayer so you can be guided to make the best decisions.

A Hard Decision

While we were on vacation, our daughter fell off a bunk bed and broke her jaw in two places. Her bottom teeth twisted, going the opposite direction; she had a gash under her chin and a sprained wrist. We praised God that she did not have any permanent injury such as brain damage, paralysis, or loss of life. After eating through a thin syringe for a few months, she was finally better. But we needed to find an oral surgeon to take off the wires that had wired her jaw shut. We did not know anyone, so we prayed that God would guide us to the right one. We checked our insurance and narrowed it down to two names. One surgeon had twenty years' experience; the other had only five years' experience. Both were qualified. The one with less experience was a Christian; both had good reputations. But we did not want to choose the Christian doctor just because he was a believer. So we prayed again for wisdom. God brought to my mind the time that He chose David to be king of Israel. He was just a boy, but God did not choose him because of his stature or outward appearance. God seemed to say to me that He would give the one with less experience the wisdom he needed to help our daughter. So we chose him by faith. We found out later that he had been more recently trained in the newest technology. The more experienced doctor had been telling us that she would have to have a root canal and have her jaw broken again later. But the younger doctor knew because of a new discovery that she would not have to have any root canals or her jaw broken again. There were other ways to help her. We would have caused our daughter unnecessary pain and suffering and had a lot more expense if we had not prayed for wisdom. We learned it does mean that God's ways are not our ways. (And He always knows the updates!) He says in Isaiah 55:8-9, "For My thoughts are not your thoughts, nor are your ways My ways, says the LORD. For as the heavens are higher than the earth, so are My ways higher than your ways, and My thoughts than your thoughts." Thank God, we prayed for wisdom and listened to God this time. We need to always ask God <u>first</u> because He knows more than we do about every situation. Acquiring knowledge through universities, family, the internet, or other ways could be helpful, but we can be deceived by other knowledge unless we balance it with prayer and God's Word. The *words out of God's mouth (Bible)* will give you the best wisdom, knowledge, and understanding. Pray for wisdom, and you will have more success.

DAY 3
Choosing the Right Path

Memorization and Testimony: Try playing a memory game today.

1. **Jeremiah 29:11** "For I know the thoughts that I think toward you, says the LORD, thoughts of peace and not of evil, to give you a future and a hope."

2. **Romans 12:1-2** "I beseech you therefore, brethren, by the mercies of God, that you present your bodies a living sacrifice, holy, acceptable to God, which is your reasonable service. And do not be conformed to this world, but be transformed by the renewing of your mind, that you may prove what is that good and acceptable and perfect will of God."

3. **Testimony** – Share your testimony with a friend or family member this week.

   Books of the Bible: Review reciting Matthew through 1 and 2 Timothy. Now say Titus, Philemon, Hebrews, James, 1st and 2nd Peter, 1st and 2nd and 3rd John, Jude, and Revelation.

Dear Jesus, thank You for designing the path that is best for me. I know I can trust You totally. Please help me to be open to the instructions in Your Word and the purpose You have for me. Lead me to follow the right path daily and in the future. In Jesus' name, Amen.

The Right Path

Address Error
Consider the case of the Illinois man who left the snow-filled streets of Chicago for a vacation in Florida. His wife was on a business trip and was planning to meet him there the next day. When he reached his hotel, he decided to send his wife a quick email. Unfortunately, when typing her address, he missed one letter, and his note was directed instead to an elderly preacher's wife whose husband had passed away only the day before. When the grieving widow checked her email, she took one look at the monitor, screamed, and fell to the floor in a dead faint. At the sound, her family rushed into the room and saw this note on the screen: "Dearest wife: Just got checked in. Everything prepared for your arrival tomorrow. P.S. Sure is hot down here."[1]

Even though that story is humorous, we all realize we need to make sure we have the correct address when traveling on God's highway of life. If you follow God's map, the Word of God, you will have the correct address for the right road in life. But if you look to other people or sources that are not in line with God's Word, you will steer off course, end up going down a wrong road, and have wrecks in your life. This can cause you to miss God's best for your life for a day, week, month, or even years. It is your choice. Remember that all it takes to get back on track is to follow God's Word and do what He says. You will have less heartache and fewer consequences and more joy and peace when you obey God.

Now that you know where to get wisdom to make the best decisions, you are on the road to finding God's wonderful plan and purpose for your life! How do you want your life to turn out? Do you want to be fulfilled in what you do? _____ If you want to become what you were made to be, that would lead to fulfillment. Why? Because you are being and doing what your Master Designer intended. You must be willing to follow His directions from His map for your life. Anything else leads to disappointment, misery, sadness, and unfulfillment. For true success, get out the Bible, the perfect map, and consult the Author, Jesus Christ. He is your Wonderful Counselor, Father, and Lord!

- **What is God's Purpose for Me as His Child?**

Before you can go down the right road of life, you must know the purpose of your trip. Is it to be happy, rich, or fulfilled? Let's find out. Read each verse, answering the questions, and write down what God's purpose is for you from each verse.

1. Look up **Mark 12:30**—What does God want you to do more than anything else? _____
    _____

2. Corinthians 6:20 says, "For you were bought at a price; therefore glorify God in your body and in your spirit, which are God's." When Jesus made you and paid for you with His blood, you were His. What is His main purpose for your life? _____
    _____

3. Look up **Colossians 1:18**. Who is to be first place in your life? _____

4. Psalm 150:6 says "Let everything that has breath praise the LORD. Praise the LORD!"
    What is the job of every creature? _____

5. Look up **Matthew 5:16.** What evidence is to stand out in you so God will look great to others? _____

God's utmost desire is for us to *love Him with all our heart, soul, mind, and strength.* That is not a selfish request. God knows that when we love Him more than anything or anybody, we will then love our neighbor as our self. When these two things happen, we will *glorify God* in our body and spirit and obey Him more and be blessed. This is *putting God in first place* as most important in our life. Then we will *praise the LORD* (brag on Him with our words and life), and that is why we were created. This in turn brings more people to Jesus Christ's kingdom because *our light, God's light in us (our good works)* will shine to the world. They will see an evidence of God in us, a difference, and want what we have. God's plan is perfect for us and all other people in the world. That is because He is so good and perfectly holy. Doing things God's way is the only way for true success in every area of life.

6. What is the spiritual fruit God desires to produce through you? (See the following verses.)

_____

John 15:8 says, "By this My Father is glorified, that you bear much fruit; so you will be My disciples."

Galatians 5:22-23 says, "But the fruit of the Spirit is love, joy, peace, longsuffering, kindness, goodness, faithfulness, gentleness, self-control. Against such there is no law."

2 Peter 1:5-7 says, "But also for this very reason, giving all diligence, add to your faith virtue, to virtue knowledge, to knowledge self-control, to self-control perseverance, to perseverance godliness, to godliness brotherly kindness, and to brotherly kindness love."

Proverbs 11:30 says, "The fruit of the righteous is a tree of life, and he who wins souls is wise."

According to all of the verses in number six, what brings God glory, honors Him, and magnifies Him? _____

_____

The fruit of God's character takes time to produce. The longer you know Jesus and spend time with Him in His Word (John 15:5) and pray that He helps you obey Him, you will produce the qualities of His character like *love, joy, peace, patience, kindness, goodness, faithfulness, gentleness, and self-control*, as well as the characteristic of *leading other people to be born into God's family*. It honors God for you to *bear much spiritual fruit*. Producing godly attitudes and deeds happens only when we are planted in the rich soil of God's Word.

7. Psalm 92:13-14 says, "Those who are planted in the house of the LORD shall flourish in the courts of our God. They shall still bear fruit in old age; they shall be fresh and flourishing." Where can you find rich soil to help you be healthy spiritually in order to produce more spiritual fruit? _____

When you are faithful in attending *a Bible-believing church*, you are able to get more teaching from *God's Word* and fellowship with other believers. These resources encourage you and will help you continue to produce spiritual fruit and fulfill one of the purposes God has for you. He gives you joy when you obey Him and become more like God as you apply His Word to your life. He is not interested in making you rich or happy. You are already rich in His love and in the many gifts He has given you at salvation and gives you every day. You will have joy when you spend time with God, and that is better than temporary happiness. Tomorrow, learn how God's purpose intertwines with His specific plan for you.

DAY 4
Following the Right Plan

Memorization and Testimony: Try another memory game today. (See appendix for ideas.)

1. **Jeremiah 29:11** "For I know the thoughts that I think toward you, says the LORD, thoughts of peace and not of evil, to give you a future and a hope."

2. **Romans 12:1-2** "I beseech you therefore, brethren, by the mercies of God, that you present your bodies a living sacrifice, holy, acceptable to God, which is your reasonable service. And do not be conformed to this world, but be transformed by the renewing of your mind, that you may prove what is that good and acceptable and perfect will of God."

3. **Testimony** – Have you shared your testimony with a friend or family member this week?

   Books of the Bible: Review reciting Matthew through 1 and 2 Timothy. Now say Titus, Philemon, Hebrews, James, 1st and 2nd Peter, 1st and 2nd and 3rd John, Jude, and Revelation.

Lord, thank You for being my Wonderful Counselor. Help my heart to be submissive to Your will today, trusting You in all areas. Guide me to be open to the best plan You have for me each day. In Jesus' name, Amen.

- **What is God's Plan for My Life?**

To have this question answered, you must be willing to obey God in <u>every area</u> of your life. This is <u>not</u> the same as promising to be perfect. This simply means you are allowing Jesus to be the Boss of your life. Trust that He knows what is best for you. After all, God is an all-wise God Who created the whole world, including you, with a perfect plan in mind for your life.

Obeying God is NOT following a bunch of religious rules. It IS knowing that your Heavenly Father loves you, and His instructions to you will keep you safe from evil and put you on the path to successful living. "For this is the love of God, that we keep his commandments. And his commandments are not burdensome" (1 John 5:3).

> God has a bigger plan for me than I have for myself!

Beware! You may be tempted to listen to lies that trick you into not following God's perfect plan and purpose for your life. One lie may come in your thoughts, saying, "If I go my way, I will be happier; if I go God's way, I will be bored, unhappy, miserable, and not have any fun. I will live like a monk and be in bondage." But that is all a lie! The exact opposite is true!

Jim Elliot, missionary to the Auca Indians in Ecuador, said, "He is no fool who gives what he cannot keep to gain that which he cannot lose."[2] You cannot lose when you give it all to God. Remember the purpose for which God created you? When you are truly saved, you will have a love for God and an attitude of gratitude for the gifts He has given you. You will want to love and glorify Him, put Him in first place, praise Him, perform good deeds, and become more like Him. Then you will truly be His disciple. When you follow His purpose, you will accomplish His plan.

1.   Read **Psalm 37:4.** What does God tell you to do in order to acquire your desires? _____

_____

If you delight in God only to get the things you want, would that be really delighting <u>in God</u>? _____ When you truly *delight in God,* <u>your desires will become His desires</u>. How do you motivate yourself to delight in God that much? Your motivation will come from obedience, spending so much time in His Word that His thoughts will become more in line with your thoughts. Have you ever been around someone so much that you started picking up that person's mannerisms and maybe voice inflections or expressions? _____When we "hang out" (spend time) with God, we will become more like Him. That is why He can give you what your heart desires as an added blessing. Your desires will match His desires. You will obey Him more, and you will be blessed more and more abundantly!

The Blessings of Obedience

One day I was studying the blessings of obedience. I knew that obeying God was not a thing to be dreaded. God called us all to obey Him because He knows what is best. Just as children need to obey their earthly parents because parents know how to keep children safe, well, and happy, God knows even more; He knows the answers to all of life's questions. He knows how to keep us all safe from evil and how to steer us on the right path to success. So I looked up verses on obedience. I was so overwhelmed with joy as I was studying this topic that I had to share it with my daughter, who was only about eight years old at the time. I shared with her some of the blessings of obedience, such as protection, joy, avoidance of evil, peace, favor with God and man, and so on. She got so encouraged that she said, "Mommy, I think I need to be baptized." She had been afraid to get into the water in front of all those people at church. I had not recently said anything to her about it. I knew that she needed to grow in her faith and love for God, and she would want to do that some day when she was ready. She would learn she did not need to be afraid anymore. She came up with this decision on her own. She was baptized on Easter Sunday that year. She learned that when we realize how good God is, we do not have to let fear stand in the way of obeying Him in any area! He wants what is best for us. Her love for God overcame her fears. "Perfect love casts out fear" (1 John 4:18b).

2. Is there an area in which you have been struggling to obey God? _____
   What is it?_____

Are you afraid if you obey God in that area that something bad will happen? _____
Instead, we need to be afraid to disobey God. There are many consequences of not following God.
When we obey Him, we may have to make some sacrifices. But these are worth it. They are nothing
compared with the problems we will have if we continue to disobey God. You and I must decide
whose team we are on. Is it the devil's team or God's team? _____
_____ There is no other team to choose from. Joshua decided for his
house, and you should decide for yourself. You should also be the leader in your family if you are
the husband/father or the only parent. If you are the mother and married, you can be a leader for
your children until your husband comes to that place. But make room for your husband to lead
when he is around. If you are single, now is the time to establish the habit of loving God through
obedience. Actions speak louder than words and prove what our words are saying. Obedience is
always the best choice. You can say what Joshua said. "Choose for yourselves this day whom you
will serve…. But as for me and my house, we will serve the LORD" (Joshua 24:15b and c). Choosing
to obey God will bring about blessings in your life and enable you to reach the potential He has
given you. You will want to obey God when you are in love with Him. Pray now that God will
help you be willing to obey His plan of obedience and trust that He knows what is best. He loves
you more than you love yourself!

Dear Jesus,

*Thank You for loving me with a perfect love. Please forgive me for not trusting You enough with all
my life decisions. Help me to obey You in everything, especially in the area I am afraid to trust You in
which is _____.*

*I give this fear to You because I know You love me more than anyone ever could and want what is best
for me. Thank You that You know my future and have a wonderful plan for my life. Help me to not
worry, but to trust You with every decision. I love You!*

In Jesus' name, Amen.

DAY 5
The Love Gift

<u>Memorization and Testimony</u>: Try another memory game today or say five times.

1. <u>Jeremiah 29:11</u> "For I know the thoughts that I think toward you, says the LORD, thoughts of peace and not of evil, to give you a future and a hope."

2. <u>Romans 12:1-2</u> "I beseech you therefore, brethren, by the mercies of God, that you present your bodies a living sacrifice, holy, acceptable to God, which is your reasonable service. And do not be conformed to this world, but be transformed by the renewing of your mind, that you may prove what is that good and acceptable and perfect will of God."

3. <u>Testimony</u> – Have you shared your testimony with a friend or family member this week?

   <u>Books of the Bible</u>: Review reciting Matthew through 1 and 2 Timothy. Now say Titus, Philemon, Hebrews, James, 1st and 2nd Peter, 1st and 2nd and 3rd John, Jude, and Revelation.

Lord Jesus, thank You for putting me first before Yourself. Please cleanse me of any wrong attitudes, deeds, or fears. Open my eyes so I will not be distracted from the truths You desire to teach me today. Help me to be obedient to You out of a grateful heart of love and that I will put You first place in every area of my life. In Jesus' name, Amen.

- **What Gift does God want from Me?**

Have You Ever Been in Love?

A lady tells of a time when she was first in love with her husband-to-be. She was so excited because she wanted to give him a surprise coat for Christmas. It was a huge sacrifice for her to buy it, but she did not care about that. She just wanted to surprise him and give him something special. When you are in love, you want to give to the other person. As you realize how much Jesus loves you, you will want to give a gift back to God. The gift He wants from you does not cost any money. It does not hurt you at all; it actually helps you. It is the gift of YOU! God's Word says:

I surrender all!

"I beseech you therefore, brethren, by the mercies of God, that you present your bodies a living sacrifice, holy, acceptable to God, which is your reasonable service. And do not be conformed to this world, but be transformed by the renewing of your mind, that you may prove what is that good and acceptable and perfect will of God" (Romans 12:1-2). The gift of giving yourself to God is <u>not</u> a promise to be perfect. It is simply a <u>gift of love from your heart, a commitment to keep working toward obedience, a decision to put Jesus in first place in all areas of your life.</u> God understands that humans are imperfect beings. As you give yourself to Him, you are saying that you want to go God's way instead of the way of the world. It will be exciting to learn about His plan for you. Jesus said, "I am come that they may have life, and that they may have it more abundantly" (John 10:10b). It will not be a burden to obey God when you love Him. Obedience shows you are truly a child of God. According to Romans 12:1-2 (above), why do you need to give a gift of yourself back to God? _____

Since God gave Himself as a free gift for you, giving yourself to Him *is your reasonable service.* This will help you grow closer to God and accomplish His wonderful plan for your life. Will you give yourself as a gift of love and gratitude to Him? _____

Three Kings give us an example of obedience, but we will learn about two of them today.

- **King David:** Read **1 Chronicles 29:5-9**. What question did King David ask the people in verse five? _____

"Consecrate" means "to be full of, accomplish, give in, set, labor, ministry, service, swear (meaning to promise, not say swear words), yield." When *he asked the people to consecrate themselves to God,* He was asking who was willing to give themselves to be yielded to God's will in their life and to serve Him with all their heart. The people showed the yielded attitude in their hearts by their outward actions of giving to help build the temple. **Look in verse 9.** Did King David or anyone else force them give to the Lord? _____ How do you know? _____

When *they gave willingly,* that meant of their own free will. When you willingly give, that is true giving. I do not know about you, but I do not want anyone to be my friend or to love me because someone <u>makes</u> him or her love me. Do you? _____ God does not want us to be made to love Him either. That is why He gave us all a free choice to sin or not, to accept Him as Savior or not, and to give our lives to Him or not. Since He has already proved His love by saving us from our sins, would He make us miserable if we decided to love Him back? No, of course not. What emotion did the people and King David experience in **verse 9** as a result of consecrating (giving themselves) to the Lord? _____ Was it just a little *joy* or a lot? _____ God always blesses us with joy and peace when we are obeying Him! We may have to sacrifice for the one we love. We may even go through some pain. But when you are in love, that is a small price to pay, isn't it? _____

- **King Jehoshaphat:** See **2 Chronicles 17:1-13**. Did King Jehoshaphat, who was a descendant of King David, decide to believe and worship the false gods of the Baals or the God of Israel, our Messiah Jesus? _____ What three ways did God bless him in verse five? _____
  _____
  _____

When King Jehoshaphat decided to believe and worship *the Lord*, God blessed him by *establishing his kingdom*, causing *all of Judah to give him presents*, and giving him *riches and honor in abundance*. God does not make your life miserable when you decide to love and obey Him. He blesses you in a variety of ways!

In order to serve God, we need to take a stand against sin. When King Jehoshaphat decided to give his heart to the true God (verse 6), what did he get rid of in Judah? _____

_____

He *removed all kinds of idol worship* in his kingdom. If we are going to serve God, we need to make sure our lives, our homes, and our children are cleansed of evil too. We cannot say we love God totally and allow sin to continue where our flesh is in charge. How did the king influence others in verse 9? _____

God sent the king's leaders (verses 7-9) to help him *teach the people the Word of God*. When we love God, we will also want to help others know Him more. We should study God's Word ourselves and pass that love and desire down to our families, especially our children. It should overflow to others outside our family that we come in contact with too. When we know good news, we cannot wait to let others in on it. Because the Word of God was being taught to the people, they began to fear the Lord (verse 10). That meant they started to respect God and His Word. As a result, how did God protect and bless the king in verses 10-13? _____

_____

_____

God protected Jehoshaphat by *causing the kingdoms around him to be afraid of him and not to make war with him*. God caused *the Philistines and Arabians to give him presents, animals, and more property,* all of which *made him more powerful*. God also *sent him men of war and mighty men of valor* in Jerusalem and in other cities throughout Judah to protect him and his kingdom. His obedience to God brought peace to his land. When we totally obey God, He will bring peace to our lives, our families, and our land too. Tomorrow, find out what happened to the third king.

DAY 6
My Best Gift

Memorization and Testimony: Say the others five times each, then say them to a friend.

1. **Jeremiah 29:11** "For I know the thoughts that I think toward you, says the LORD, thoughts of peace and not of evil, to give you a future and a hope."

2. **Romans 12:1-2** "I beseech you therefore, brethren, by the mercies of God, that you present your bodies a living sacrifice, holy, acceptable to God, which is your reasonable service. And do not be conformed to this world, but be transformed by the renewing of your mind, that you may prove what is that good and acceptable and perfect will of God."

3. **Testimony** – Today is your last chance to share your testimony this week.

   Books of the Bible: Review reciting Matthew through 1 and 2 Timothy. Now say Titus, Philemon, Hebrews, James, 1st and 2nd Peter, 1st and 2nd and 3rd John, Jude, and Revelation.

Father God, thank You for Your perfect love and faithfulness to me every day. I do not deserve it. Please help me to be alert to the lessons from the Bible today and not be afraid to obey You in whatever You tell me. Show me how to give myself to You so I can express my gratefulness and service for all You have done for me for eternity. In Jesus' name, Amen.

Are We Products of Our Environment?

Do you think that children turn out right or wrong according to the influences around them? In the Bible, child King Josiah had an evil grandfather, Manasseh. He also had an evil father, Amon, who both "did evil in the sight of the LORD" (2 Kings 21:20a). Josiah should have been evil, right? But when he became king, 2 Kings 22:2a tells us "he did what was right in the sight of the LORD" and chose to do right even at the young age of eight years old. Maybe someone influenced him in the right ways, but he still CHOSE which way to go. When the Word of God was discovered, read how it changed everything, and look at what God said about King Josiah.

- **King Josiah:** He was a child king who decided to obey God and give himself to the Lord. It is exciting to see how God can use children when they decide to obey Him! You will enjoy reading about him.

a) Read **2 Kings 22**. Why did God decide not to bring calamity on him? (vs. 19-20) _____
_____
_____

God was going to have to punish his kingdom because of the previous sins of the people under his grandfather and father's rule. They forsook God, practiced witchcraft, performed human sacrifices, worshiped other gods, and murdered innocent people. But because Josiah was *humble* and had a *tender heart* before God, *weeping with sorrow over the sins of the people* in his kingdom, God promised to spare Josiah from seeing this judgment happen. It would be delayed until after Josiah's death. Take a few minutes to continue reading about him in 2 Kings 23 and in 2 Chronicles 34.

b) What decision did King Josiah make after reading the Word to all the people? (Read **2 Kings 23:1-3**). _____

_____

After reading the Word of God, he *made a promise to obey God with all his heart and soul, giving himself to God totally.* He gave himself as a gift back to God. Therefore, God blessed him. Josiah's actions showed the change in his heart. He cleansed his kingdom of witchcraft and idols and started leading the people to obey God's Word. Next, see what God said about him! 2 Kings 23:25 says, "Now before him there was no king like him, who turned to the LORD with all his heart, with all his soul, and with all his might, according to all the Law of Moses; nor after him did any arise like him."

> **He made the choice to obey God regardless of the evil influences in his environment.**

c) Why do you think God said this about King Josiah? _____

_____

_____

King Josiah decided to *obey God exactly.* He hated sin and got rid of witchcraft and idols in His kingdom and did not care about whether people liked him or not. He restored true worship to God and caused all the people to hear the Word of God read to them. *He made a promise to follow the LORD with all his heart and soul and all his might.* He influenced people for God faithfully all his days.

Can we be committed to God and influence others like Josiah? Yes, if a child can do it, so can we! Is love actually "real love" if we never show our love and only say we love? _____ King Josiah showed his love for God with his actions. He made the choice to obey God regardless of the evil influences in his environment. He cleansed the kingdom of sin and influenced the people to turn to obedience. Would you like the Lord Jesus to say something like this about you someday when you stand before Him? _____

The poem says it well: "Only one life, / Twill soon be past, / Only what's done for Christ will last." Philippians 1:21 says, "For to me, to live is Christ, and to die is gain."

- **How Can I Give the Gift of Myself to God?**

a) Read **1 Corinthians 3:11-15.** Who should be the foundation for our life? _____ If we give ourselves to God and determine to study His Word AND obey it, then we are building our lives on the foundation of the *Lord Jesus Christ.*

When you build a beautiful house, will it be beautiful if you use cheap materials or precious stones like gold and silver? _____When we build our lives by putting pleasures and selfish desires before God, willfully sinning, not praying to God about all decisions, not serving Him or seeking Him, or doing good works with a wrong motivation, then we are using cheap materials like wood, hay, and stubble. But when we build our lives by living for Jesus, we will store up rewards in heaven and have blessings on earth too. This is like building our life with precious stones.

b) How do you know if what you do is going to get a reward from God or if it will be a waste of your time and energy while on earth? (See verses 13-15.) _____
_____
_____

God will put your works to the *test to be revealed by fire.* The *true work for God will last* like a diamond, but *work done for our glory will be burned up.* It will reveal whether you did the good works for God or for selfish reasons; whether you worked for God or totally wasted your life. It may be possible to be a Christian, giving God only a few good works (see verse 15), but a true believer should desire to serve God. Which kind of Christian do you want to be: an embarrassed and regretful Christian, one without rewards to give to Christ, or one with rewards to give Him? _____

A Little Girl's Pearls
A little girl named Jenny saw a pearl necklace she wanted at the dime store. "May I have them? Please, Mommy, please!" Her mother looked at the price tag: $2.00. "Jenny, you could save your allowance, and since your birthday is coming up, I bet you will get some money from Grandma." Jenny was so excited. She had seventeen cents in her piggy bank to start. She worked hard doing extra chores for neighbors until she had one whole dollar. Then her birthday came, and, sure enough, Grandma gave her a crisp, new dollar bill! She hurried and bought the necklace. Jenny loved her pearl necklace. It was her favorite thing. The only time she took it off was when she took a shower or went swimming because her mother said the pearls might turn her neck green if they got wet.

One night as Jenny's loving dad read her a bedtime story, he asked Jenny, "Do you love me?" Jenny answered, "Oh, yes, Daddy. You know that I love you." "Then give me your pearls." "Oh, Daddy, not my pearls, but you can have Princess, the white horse from my collection, the one with the pink tail, the one you gave me. She's my favorite." "That's okay, Honey. Daddy loves you. Good night." And he brushed her cheek with a kiss. A week later, he asked Jenny again for her pearls as proof that she loved him. Jenny said she did love him and offered him other things that she loved. A few nights later when her daddy came in to read her a story, Jenny was sitting on her bed with her legs crossed. Her chin was trembling, and one silent tear rolled down her cheek. "What is the matter with my sweet Jenny?" Dad asked. Jenny did not answer, but lifted her hand up to her daddy. When she opened her hand, there was her little pearl necklace. With a little quiver, she finally said, "Here, Daddy. It's for you." With tears in his own eyes, Jenny's kind daddy reached out with one hand to take the dime store necklace, and with the other hand he reached into his pocket and pulled out a blue velvet case with a strand of genuine pearls and gave them to Jenny. He had them all the time. He was just waiting for her to give up the dime store necklace so he could give her a genuine treasure![3] That is what Jesus does for you and me. When we give Him our lives, our plans, our dreams, even all our desires, He turns it into something so much more valuable and useful for Him than we could ever imagine!

A Life-Changing Decision

The most important decision I made in my life was when I asked Jesus to be my Savior and Lord. The next most significant decision I made was when I decided to give myself as a gift back to God. I made this life-changing decision when I was seventeen years old. A preacher was visiting our church and was speaking on giving your life to God. That can mean different things to different people, but God was working on me on whether I would trust Him with the decision of my career in the near future. I was trying to decide

> God will choose what is BEST for you, but you have to choose first to give Him the BEST gift—yourself!

what I was supposed to do since I was going to college in the fall. I had already decided that I did not want to be a teacher. My parents had been teachers, and I had been with them when they had to stay after school every day. They also had to take papers home to grade on the weekends sometimes. That did not sound like a fun job to me. I was afraid to be a missionary since I hated bugs and roughing it and loved my free country. I had said that I would never live in Georgia, never go to a certain college in Tennessee, and never be a teacher.

But I put aside all of my preconceived ideas and worries and realized that God knew me better than I knew myself. I knew I would not have a peace about what to do with my life until I let God be in control. So I prayed right then and told God, "You can have me, all my career dreams and other desires and plans. I will be whatever You want me to be and go wherever You want me to go. I will even be a missionary or a teacher, if that is what You want for me." After that, I had a peace that was greater than all my understanding. Soon God showed me that I would really love being a teacher and later a missionary and believe it or not, go to that college in Tennessee. I even moved to Georgia later. I eventually learned to never say "never" to God. But God did <u>not</u> make me miserable in my decision. I was never happier. I loved the college. I loved teaching, and I love being a missionary. I would even pick Georgia as one of my favorite states to live in.

c) Do not believe the lie that says, "You will be miserable if you give your life to obey God." When you give your desires to God, He can change your heart to love whatever He calls you to do. He knows you better than you know yourself. Sometimes the devil will tempt you to be rebellious in an area that you would be most happy in because he is trying to hinder God's best in your life. You do not need to be afraid that your life will be miserable if you choose God's way. The enemy, the devil, wants you to think that your life will be awful and unfulfilled if you choose to give yourself to God. But that is a lie. Trust God's amazing love for you. He loves you more than anyone ever could!

d) Do you want fake, cheap pearls or real pearls? _____
God will choose what is BEST for you, but you have to choose first to give Him the BEST gift: yourself.

You may or may not have already chosen a career, a college, or a mate. But no matter what age you are or what decisions you have left to make for the future, why not make sure you are starting out on the right foot with God? If you do not remember a day when you told God you will give Him all your desires and plans, your whole self, why don't you do that right now? Tell Him that He can have YOU TOTALLY! Do not let fear get in the way. You cannot begin to REALLY LIVE until you give yourself to God, not only once, but daily. It should be natural to give yourself as a gift back to God. It may be hard, but God will reward you for submitting to Him and allowing the Holy Spirit to control you (Eph. 5:18). It will start as a decision today, but continue as an ongoing experience, a decision each day of your life. Until you give yourself as a gift back to God, you cannot find God's BEST plan and blessings for your life, nor will you be able to influence as many for Christ.

> **God's plans for you are bigger than your dreams!**

e) God's plans for you are bigger than your dreams!

1 Corinthians 2:9 says, "But as it is written: 'Eye has not seen, nor ear heard, nor have entered into the heart of man the things which God has prepared for those who love Him.'" You cannot begin to have dreams big enough to match the exciting, wonderful plans God is preparing for you who love Him! Are you ready to allow God to make this verse real for you? _____ If so, pray a prayer like the following example, in your own words, and mean it from your heart.

Example Prayer:
Dear Lord Jesus,

I give myself as a gift back to You. I will go anywhere, at any time, and do anything You want me to do. Please give me the strength to obey You in every area as I grow closer to You. Help me to stay on the right path. Send me godly, Christian friends that can encourage me so I can please You and in turn help others like me some day. I love You, Jesus.

Thank You for caring about me and preparing a wonderful plan for my life. Help me to find out all the details of Your plan for me in time as I am willing to obey You. I determine to obey You one day at a time, one minute at a time. Keep me on the path to victory. Bind the devil away from me in the name and blood of Jesus Christ. I praise Your name, Jesus. You are wonderful! In Jesus' name, Amen.

Is the above prayer what you want to say to Jesus? If not, write one in your own words below. ___
_____
_____

_____

_____

Date: _____ Signature: _____

Now you are prepared to reach your fullest potential, to have the blessed life that God has planned for you! Write this date in your Bible and remember when you gave **yourself** as a gift of love back to God.

<u>Suggestion</u>: Cut out the prayer you just prayed about giving yourself as a gift back to God along with your name and the date and tape it in your Bible. What a wonderful memory.

****

Important: If you have no desire to surrender to being obedient to Christ in every area of your life, it could be you were never truly saved. It does not matter how religious you have been. If you never made Christ your Lord, then He was never really your Savior. Salvation and Lordship are one in the same (Romans 10:9). By this point in our Bible study, you have hopefully already made sure that Jesus is Lord, the Boss of your life. If you have not seen an inward and outward change in your life that shows Jesus is your Lord, that He is first place, or you are not sure, then go back and read Chapter 2 and be sure today. You can ask any questions or talk about any concerns with your teacher or pastor.

Let's review what we have learned.

XI. The Right Architect (is God)

A. God Deserves All Honor, Glory, and Power
B. Ask God for Advice First
C. Go to God's Success Manual (the Word of God)

XII. The Right Path (is going God's way)

A. What is God's Purpose for Me as His Child?
Generally, in whatever I do, I am to love God as first place in my life, glorify and praise Him, shine through producing fruits of good works and godly character, and win people to Jesus as Savior and Lord. I can only accomplish God's purpose as I faithfully continue in Bible study and attend and serve the Lord by using my spiritual gifts in my church.

B. What is God's Plan for My Life?
To follow in His steps, I must choose to delight in loving and obeying God, submitting to Him in every decision, trusting that the Lord wants the best for me and knows more than I do, and will lead me on the right path daily and in the future. If I apply these principles, I will find out what God's specific plans are for my life.

C. What Gift does God want from Me?

I am to live out His Lordship in my life through giving myself to His will in whatever He calls me to do. It is <u>not</u> a promise to be perfect. It is simply a gift of love from my heart, a commitment to keep working toward obedience, a decision to put Jesus first place in all areas of my life. When I surrender all, God will give me His best!

You are so awesome, Lord! I love You and thank You that You know what the best path is in my life. Please help me to follow the plans You have for me each day and in the future. I know I can trust You with my life, so no matter what sad or hard situations I go through, You will be with me, give me strength, and work everything together for good because You love me and have called me to fulfill Your purpose. In Jesus' name, Amen.

CHAPTER 6
Watching Out for the Main Tricks of My Enemy: Tricks 1-4

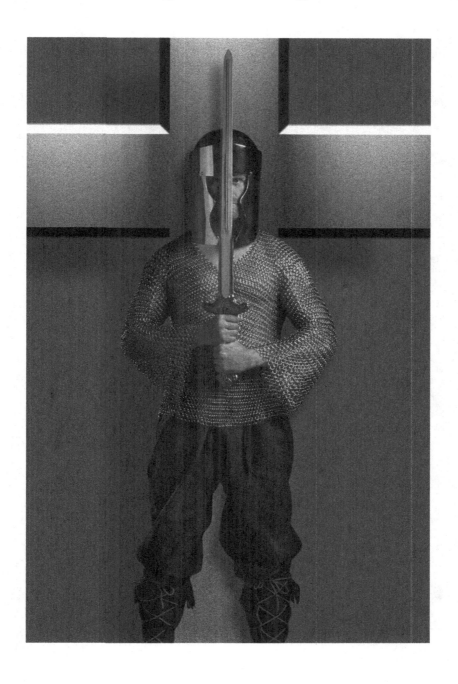

DAY 1
Forming Healthy Habits

Memorization and Testimony: Say the verses and Gospel points five times and be prepared to share your testimony.

1. **Hebrews 10:25** – "Not forsaking the assembling of ourselves together, as is the manner of some, but exhorting one another, and so much the more as you see the Day approaching."

2. **Matthew 28:19-20** – "Go therefore and make disciples of all the nations, baptizing them in the name of the Father and of the Son and of the Holy Spirit, teaching them to observe all things that I have commanded you; and lo, I am with you always, even to the end of the age. Amen."

3. **GP7**: Share assurance. (Rom. 10:9-13; Heb. 13:5-6; John 1:12)

4. **GP8**: Share 6 growth steps: 1. Pray daily. 2. Read and obey Bible daily. 3. Go to church weekly. 4. Be baptized. 5. Witness 6. Confess sin. (1 Jn. 1:9; 2 Peter 3:18; 1 Jn. 2:28)

5. **GP9**: Tell someone now what God has done for you. **T**ract, **A**ddress, **P**rayer (Matt. 10:32-33; 1 John 2:22-23)

6. **Share your testimony (and Lead-in and Response questions)** with a co-worker or neighbor this week.

Father God, thank You for your patience with me. Work in me today to become more committed to You by learning the spiritual disciplines I need in my life to be successful as You planned for me to be. In Jesus' name, Amen.

Form Spiritual Disciplines

What kind of habits do you perform each day in order to stay alive? Do you eat nutritious food, drink clean water, get sleep, and exercise? The only time a person would not perform these normal habits is if he or she were sick or had passed away. As a Christian, if we do not form habits that keep us spiritually healthy, then we can become spiritually sick. This comes from disobedience and unconfessed sin in our hearts. It will keep us from being disciplined enough to get the spiritual nutrition we need to be strong in the Lord. Following are some of the spiritual disciplines that you need to stay healthy and productive as a Christian. The first four are essential to your success in life. If you allow the devil to deceive you from being successful in any of these four areas, you are simply starving yourself spiritually. As a result, you will not have very many victories, joy, peace, or strength in your life. What are these tricks?

- **Trick 1: The Enemy will try to Stop You from Reading Your Bible and Praying**

Reading God's Word is like eating a spiritual meal. You must have it daily! Decide on a daily time and stick to it. Read **John 15:4-6.** What will you be unable to do if you do not abide, that is, spend time with Christ in His Word each day? (vs. 4) _____
_____ One of the purposes of being a Christian is to *produce spiritual fruit* such as love, joy, peace, patience, gentleness, goodness, faith, meekness, self-control, and to be able to lead people to Jesus. You would be hindering the very reason you were created if you did not read and study God's Word and grow in these qualities.

What happens when we stay connected to God in His Word (see vs. 5)? _____
_____ If a plant is not connected to the vine, what will happen to it (vs. 6)? _____ If we are not connected to Jesus, the True Vine, what will happen to us spiritually (vs. 6)? _____
_____

When we stay connected to God's Word daily, we will *bear much fruit* in our lives. We will become more like Jesus. When a plant is not connected to the vine, it ceases to get the nourishment it needs. It will *wither and die.* As believers, if we do not stay connected to God through His Word and church, *our influence will wither and we will not grow spiritually.* If we try to live the Christian life through our own strength, *we will fail.* God will not be able to use us in that state until we become connected to Him again. But as believers, we have the Holy Spirit inside us to give us strength, so we must feed our new nature by being connected to our nourishment source: Jesus Christ, the Word! True believers will live a lifestyle of obeying God because they spend time learning from God's Word through personal Bible study and in church. An unsaved person does not desire to abide (spend time listening and learning) in God's Word. The life of an unbeliever shows he or she is not changed spiritually. Unbelievers will be *burned in the everlasting fire in hell* unless they become a new creature by becoming God's children. But those who are God's children and regularly spend time in His Word become closer to God and more like Jesus. As a result, they will sin less and less and live a lifestyle of obedience by continuing to be faithful to follow God.

The Tomato Plant Miracle

As a child, I accidentally knocked over my mother's tomato plant with a ball. As a result, it was barely connected together. I was worried that I would get in big trouble with my mother, so I grabbed some masking tape and taped the broken plant back together. I prayed that it would keep growing and not die. After a week or so, I realized a miracle had happened. It did not die, but kept growing and produced tomatoes! It was probably the first plant surgery performed by a child. With help from God, that plant continued living and growing because it actually stayed connected to its stem, even though it was barely connected with tape.

When you choose to sin, you do not stay connected to your Savior. He is not going to stretch out any tape and repair your lost connection. You must choose to stay connected to Him; then He will honor His Word and give you the spiritual nourishment to live for Him. But when you do not make it a priority to spend time with Him or pray, you are denying His help and wisdom; you are not relying on the power of God during that time.

If the tomato plant had kept growing but did not produce any tomatoes, it might as well have died. Why? Because producing tomatoes was its main purpose for being a tomato plant. What good is a tomato plant without tomatoes? So what good is a Christian if he does not produce spiritual fruit to draw people to Christ and fulfill God's purpose for being on earth as His child? Will you have the spiritual strength and nourishment to do anything for Christ without abiding close to Him in His Word? _____ Write the last phrase in **John 15:5**. _____

_____

We must give all glory to God, and as He is lifted up in the earth, what will happen? (Read **John 12:32**.) _____

We *cannot do anything without God*. The fruit of the Spirit glorifies God by *drawing people to the Savior*. It lifts up Jesus when you live for Him and shine His attitudes toward others in the world. Then they can see what Jesus is like through your flesh living out the actions and deeds that reflect Christ. The ultimate fruit that you can produce is <u>to reproduce yourself by leading someone else to be saved and discipling him or her</u> so he or she grows spiritually!

Are you a grandparent, mom, dad, a son, or daughter? _____ Are you a boss or employee? _____ Are you a neighbor? _____ Your testimony of obedience to God can bring others to Christ! Your lack of obeying God will influence your family and co-workers and neighbors in a negative way. Another person's changed life is one of the best reasons to stay faithful to studying God's Word. Then you can have a part in being on God's rescue team as you help rescue people from the punishment of hell and guide them into the wonderful presence of God on earth as they learn to walk daily with Him and be in heaven someday. Do you see how important it is to stay in tune with God through His Word? _____

When you eat enough physical food and ingest the proper nutrients, your body will not get sick as often, but have enough energy to do what you need to do. It is the same way spiritually. Are you becoming more consistent in ingesting God's Word into your heart and mind? _____ If so, you will become a healthy Christian, one who develops a strong spiritual immune system that will recognize and fight off the devil's tricks and avoid spiritual sickness. You will be able to have the spiritual energy to do all God has planned for your life and influence others in a positive way. Then you will defeat the devil more often!

DAY 2
Becoming a Healthy Christian

Memorization and Testimony: Say the memory verses and Gospel points five times.

1. **Hebrews 10:25** – "Not forsaking the assembling of ourselves together, as is the manner of some, but exhorting one another, and so much the more as you see the Day approaching."

2. **Matthew 28:19-20** – "Go therefore and make disciples of all the nations, baptizing them in the name of the Father and of the Son and of the Holy Spirit, teaching them to observe all things that I have commanded you; and lo, I am with you always, even to the end of the age. Amen."

3. **GP7**: Share assurance. (Rom. 10:9-13; Heb. 13:5-6; John 1:12)

4. **GP8**: Share 6 growth steps: 1. Pray daily. 2. Read and obey Bible daily. 3. Go to church weekly. 4. Be baptized. 5. Witness 6. Confess sin. (1 Jn. 1:9; 2 Peter 3:18; 1 Jn. 2:28)

5. **GP9**: Tell someone now what God has done for you. **T**ract, **A**ddress, **P**rayer (Matt. 10:32-33; 1 John 2:22-23)

6. **Share your testimony (and Lead-in and Response questions)** with a co-worker or neighbor this week.

Lord, sometimes sin tries to trick me in my mind, through the culture, or people near me. Show me how to be wise and recognize the tricks of sin so I will not fail. Thank You for being my Victor! Please cleanse me and give me joy in Your Word today. Help me to be obedient and disciplined so I can reach the exciting path You have laid out for me. In Jesus' name, Amen.

It Tastes Good!

Have you ever tasted a food when you were older that you thought you hated when you were a child? But when you tried it later, you realized it tasted great. There is another kind of food we need to taste. It is the Word of God. The devil tries to make us think we will not enjoy the Bible, but that is a lie! Psalm 34:8a says, "Oh, taste and see that the LORD is good." Enjoy the taste of God's Word to get the spiritual nutrition you need today. Read **John 15:7**. What is a big key in having your prayers answered according to this verse? _____

It is pleasing to God for you to *abide* (spend time) *with God through His Word and let* His words abide in you, that is, *memorizing His Word* so it is in your heart and mind. He agrees to answer your prayers when you do it. Why do you think God makes this promise? _____

_____

When you spend a lot of time with a person, you become like that person. God knows that if you spend time with Him, *your desires will start matching with God's desires and your prayers will be in line with His will.* You will not pray a prayer that is against His will when you spend a lot of time with Him.

Prayer is like breathing or drinking water. You cannot get very far in the Christian life without it. Could you get very close to any friend if you talked to the friend only when you needed help? _____ Friendships are kept close by a lot of communication. We must communicate with our Heavenly Father to draw closer to Him. God works through your prayers to glorify Himself, to save lives, physically and spiritually, heal the sick, solve problems, give you joy, and to meet any need you may have. If we abide in Him, we can ask God whatever we desire, and we will receive it! Do you want your prayers answered like that? _____

Read **John 14:13-14**. What does God promise to you when you pray to Him "in His name"? _____
_____ This verse not only means praying to God by beginning or ending the prayer in "Jesus' name, Amen." It also means asking God for your requests "in His will." Simply, it means if your prayer goes along with His plan and purpose for you, others, and the world, then *He will do it. It will be answered* so God may be glorified through His Son Jesus for answering your prayer. Of course, you must also believe in your heart that God will answer it. If God has a better plan than what you requested, then He will answer either "no" or "wait." He always answers what is right and best. We need to trust and know that God's ways are not always our ways, and His ways and timing are best even when our human minds cannot understand. Just as a loving parent will never turn away a genuine need the child has, so your Heavenly Father will never turn away a real need you have if you will ask Him in the <u>name of Jesus</u> (in God's will), believing He will answer you.

The Flying Car

We were traveling back from a vacation when we heard a popping sound. My husband looked in his mirror and saw that the jeep behind us on the highway had just been hit. It was twirling in the air extremely fast and flying toward us at the same time! He stepped on the gas harder. I looked back and I knew that no one would survive that kind of wreck unless it was a miracle of God. I prayed immediately that all their lives would be saved, that God would comfort them and send help, and that He would save those who did not know the Lord as Savior. When we stopped, I grabbed a blanket and ran beside the highway back to the location of the wreck. It was dusk, and my vision was hindered because of the lights of the other cars. As I sprinted about a half a mile back, I prayed for protection from snakes in the high grass and holes so I could get there safely to help them.

When I arrived, there were many people who had stopped to help. I saw that God had answered my prayer, and everyone was alive. That was a miracle! But their jeep was upside down, and the mother was still lying in the car. I told her that God had sent many people to help her and that everyone was alive and awake. I asked her if she knew Jesus as her Savior and she did. She was hurt badly with a gash in her head and hand, but I prayed for her and then the paramedics arrived. Her two daughters were shaken up, but did not appear to be hurt badly. Another girl was lying on a side road running parallel to the highway. She must have been thrown from the car. A man told me that cars were coming down that road trying to get around the traffic, and they would have hit her, but he was standing in the street and they saw him. I believe God sent him to protect that girl because of my prayer to save their lives. A sixteen-year-old girl was lying down and barely conscious. I talked to her to try to get her to respond to prevent her from going into a coma or dying. Her leg was ripped open from the middle of her thigh to the middle of her shin with most of the blood gone. It did not look good. After I kept speaking to her, she became more alert. I told her that Jesus loved her and if she would ask Him to help her, He would. The only verse that came to my mind at that moment was John 14:14: "If you ask anything in My name, I will do it." I quoted it and shared with her that she could call on Jesus' name to help her through this situation and forgive her of her sins. He promised to answer her call if she called on His name. She asked me, "He wouldn't forgive my sin, would He?" I said, "Oh, yes, He will. He loves you and He always keeps His promises." I saw her lips moving and a peace that passed through her face. Then the paramedics came to attend to her. God answered my prayer for lives to be saved physically and one spiritually.

When you read, memorize, and use the power of God's Word and prayer in your life, you can share it and God will use it in others' lives as well. Be sure to study the Bible and pray to Him on a regular basis. Then you will be prepared to help yourself and others too. The daily reading of <u>God's Word and prayer</u> are THE MOST IMPORTANT TWO HABITS you need to do in order to reach your potential to be all God wants you to be. This is where your greatest blessings and greatest victories will come from.

Next, you must learn to <u>live your life by making your decisions based on the Word of God</u>. This is called developing a biblical worldview. Did you know that only 9% of people who call themselves Christians have a biblical worldview?[1] This means they believe the basic beliefs about God for salvation from the Bible. The other 91% are being tricked or may not be true Christians in the first place. Or maybe no one taught them the truths about God and the way to honor God and be successful. The devil tricks Christians by getting them to live by their emotions (what feels right), instead of by the truth of God's Word. But you have a choice. Whenever you make a decision, are hurt, or confused, go to the Word of God first. The Bible says it is the *"truth that will set you free."* Are you being tricked by neglecting Bible reading or prayer? Pray for God to help you, and He will.

DAY 3
Eating at God's House

Memorization and Testimony: Try a memory game and recite the Gospel points five times.

1. <u>Hebrews 10:25</u> – "Not forsaking the assembling of ourselves together, as is the manner of some, but exhorting one another, and so much the more as you see the Day approaching."

2. <u>Matthew 28:19-20</u> – "Go therefore and make disciples of all the nations, baptizing them in the name of the Father and of the Son and of the Holy Spirit, teaching them to observe all things that I have commanded you; and lo, I am with you always, even to the end of the age. Amen."

3. <u>GP7</u>: Share assurance. (Rom. 10:9-13; Heb. 13:5-6; John 1:12)

4. <u>GP8</u>: Share 6 growth steps: 1. Pray daily. 2. Read and obey Bible daily. 3. Go to church weekly. 4. Be baptized. 5. Witness 6. Confess sin. (1 Jn. 1:9; 2 Peter 3:18; 1 Jn. 2:28)

5. <u>GP9</u>: Tell someone now what God has done for you. **Tract, Address, Prayer** (Matt. 10:32-33; 1 John 2:22-23)

6. <u>**Share your testimony (and Lead-in and Response questions)**</u> with a co-worker or neighbor this week.

Jesus, thank You that I can spend time with You through the Bible and prayer. Help me not to be tricked in that area. Now open my eyes to be prepared to have victory in this next area and help me to obey You faithfully. In Jesus' name, Amen.

Now that you know the first trick which is neglecting the reading of God's Word and prayer, be ready for the next trick:

*   **Trick 2: The Enemy will try to Keep You out of Church and Small Group Bible Study as much as Possible.**

Grandmother's House

When we went to eat at my grandparents' house, it gave me such a good feeling. It was a tiny, cozy house, and the food was delicious, but the best part was being with my grandparents. There is something special about going to the house of someone you really love. As believers who are in love with our Heavenly Father, we should naturally desire to go to His house. Heaven is His permanent home, but on earth we should desire to meet in a church. Read **Psalm 27:4.** What should be one of the most important desires of a true believer? _____

Churches can be in all sorts of buildings, including houses. God has invited you to eat at His house. Do you *desire to be in God's house?* When you go to church and small group Bible study, you are eating the wonderful food He has prepared for you through sermons and lessons from God's Word. It is so important to be spiritually fed from His Word in a group setting. Of course, you should read God's Word individually every day, but how can anyone turn down an invitation to God's house every week? Have you noticed it gets easier to miss another Sunday each time you miss a Sunday? The devil does not want you to be faithful to small group Bible study and church. He tricks Christians in this area because he knows that a lot of victories are won in the Christian life when you learn God's Word with other Christians in church who encourage you. Attending the right church is good for you in so many ways. It will enrich your life and strengthen you spiritually. Attending church and a small group Bible study is like:

* Going out to eat with friends: Do you grow closer to friends when you spend time with them by going out to eat? _____ Just as spending time with friends brings you closer to them, going to church brings you closer to God and other believers. All people need to be encouraged each week spiritually and socially, and being with godly friends through church functions helps strengthen your soul, your faith, and relationships. No one should be a loner in the Christian life. The church is an important support group. You were meant to be a social being that encourages, comforts, and helps others.

* Getting rest: Getting refreshed through sleep each night helps you be renewed to face the challenges of work the next day. Just as physical sleep revives you, so attending church is like getting rest spiritually from the worldly pressures. It renews you with strength, encouraging you to live the Christian life.

* Being in love: When you are in love, you enjoy thinking about how wonderful your date or spouse is, right? You may even brag on this person's qualities to a friend. When you are in love with God, you should naturally want to set aside at least one or more dates each week to brag on Him, worship His greatness, and be around other people who love Him the way you do.

There are many more advantages to going to church, which you can learn about later. But for now, you need to know that the only way God can bless you by going to church is if you find the right church for you and your family. Sometimes people can find the right church quickly, but sometimes it could take a while. But do not give up; it is worth your effort and patience. If you do not know what to look for, you may make a wrong decision.

> **There are not any perfect churches because there are not any perfect people. Remember to go to church for one main reason: Jesus!**

- **How Do I Find the Right Church Family?**

Before you go church hunting, you should know that there are not any perfect churches. Why? It is because there are not any perfect people. Remember to go to church for one main reason: Jesus! Then you will be able to overlook some things and a few people who are not friendly or loving (Proverbs 19:11). Realize that all kinds of people attend church, even non-Christians. The church is not a sanctuary for saints; it is a hospital for sinners. Go to a church that has qualities according to the Scripture, one where you can do these four things:

* Worship God (Psalm 95:6-7; Hebrews 10:25)
* Love God and others through your words and deeds (Mark 12:30-31)
* Serve God (John 12:26)
* Grow in correct Bible knowledge and in spiritual maturity (2 Peter 3:18)

All of these reasons are important. You are to worship God every day, but also set aside one day of the week in honor of Him. You need to be involved in serving God through your local church and using the spiritual gifts He has given you to use for Him. Find a church that teaches correct doctrine to help you grow spiritually more mature in Christ. You are more likely to find a loving church if you are reaching out to others in friendliness. One person said it like this: Instead of walking into a room with the attitude, "Here I am," walk in thinking, "There you are!" Proverbs 18:24a says, "A man who has friends must himself be friendly." Continue to read this devotion to find the kind of church that will be a blessing to you from God spiritually, socially, and other ways.

What are some ways people today may choose a church to attend? Check off ones you would choose:

____ The people are friendly and accepting of me and my lifestyle.
____ The sermons are not too long.
____ It has entertaining music that I really like.
____ It fits my social status.
____ It will help my reputation and could help my career.
____ It has free babysitting.
____ It has people that are the same race as I am.
____ It has a beautiful building.
____ It has a lot of activities for my family to be involved in.
____ It does not push me to give much money.
____ The sermons make me feel good. This church says it is ok to do things another church says is sin.
____ It is big enough so no one will notice if I do not get involved or miss a week or two.
____ This church goes along with social issues so they do not make non-believers feel unaccepted.

If you checked any of those reasons, then please erase them from your mind. None of those reasons are wise ways to choose a church God may want you to attend. To find out how to find the kind of church that will be a blessing to you from God spiritually, socially, and other ways, keep reading.

- **What are Some Important Qualities that a <u>Pastor</u> of a Church Should Have?**

a) Acts 17:3 says, "Explaining and demonstrating that the Christ had to suffer and rise again from the dead, and saying, 'This Jesus whom I preach to you is the Christ.'" In this verse, a pastor should _____

_____.

b) Psalm 78:72a says, "So he shepherded them according to the integrity of his heart." A pastor should show the qualities that display _____.

c) Jeremiah 3:15 says, "And I will give you shepherds according to My heart, who will feed you with knowledge and understanding." A pastor (shepherd) should _____ you with _____ and_____. Jeremiah 23:4 says, "I will set up shepherds over them who will feed them; and they shall fear no more, nor be dismayed, nor shall they be lacking, says the LORD." A pastor will feed His flock (congregation) with God's Word. If so, what needs will be met? _____

_____

What are qualities of a pastor? *(a)* He is a leader that should communicate clearly by *explaining and demonstrating the truth of the Word of God, the Gospel (death, burial, and resurrection)*, and inviting people to come to God, declaring *Jesus is the Christ (God.)* (b) He should also show how a believer lives with *integrity*, having character that reflects Christ. Look for character qualities such as: love, honesty, and humility. He should be one who stands up for the truth, protects the church in correct beliefs, has moral purity, wisdom, temperance, kindness, a consistent, growing walk with God, and other qualities like Jesus. A pastor should be an example of Christ in word and deed, having a reputation that does not hurt the name of Christ or the church. (c) He is the shepherd of the flock of God that should *feed* you and all the people by helping them grow in *knowledge* and *understanding* of the Bible so they can apply and use it to change their lives. If he is preaching the Word and led of God, the people will have more spiritual needs met such as *having faith instead of fear, trusting God for their needs instead of worrying about them*, and many other spiritual needs so they are *not lacking in growth* opportunities. If you already have a pastor like this, take time to thank him for His spiritual qualities of leadership. Continue to pray for him often so God can keep using Him to feed the flock of God.

God tells us in His Word how to have a growing church, one with the right priorities. Let's look at the example of the first church, and this will help you know what qualities to look for in a church. Even if you know you are in the place of worship God wants you to be in at this time, this may help you in the future if God ever moves you. It can also prepare you to help someone else in the search for the right church.

Read **Acts 2:40-47**. You could read the whole chapter if you like. This chapter tells when the first church started. It was successful because they did things God's way. Peter was preaching, and God produced a miracle by allowing all the people present to hear Peter's sermon in their own language, without interpreters. God made them understand in spite of language barriers. This is not necessary very often today, but was necessary at the time to start the spread of Christianity around the world. This is also when God sent the Holy Spirit to each person who believed. At this time, every believer has God, the Holy Spirit, living inside.

- **What Qualities Does a <u>Church</u> Need to Grow and be used of God in a Great Way?**

The first church was successful because the church members did things God's way. See Acts 2:40-42.

a)   (vs. 40) A church should call a pastor who will _____

_____.

b)   (vs. 40) A pastor must share the Gospel to invite people to be _____ from their sin.

c)   (vs. 41) A church should have regular _____ for those recently saved.

d)   (vs. 42) A church should faithfully teach correct _____.

e)   (vs. 42) A church should have opportunities for _____.

f)   A church should practice two ordinances: The Lord's Supper and Baptism. Which one do think verse 42 refers to here? _____

g)   (vs. 42) A church should provide opportunities for regular _____ to God as a group or congregation.

What are qualities a <u>church</u> must have? (a) A church should call a pastor who lives out a blameless *testimony, exhorting (encouraging* and *challenging)* the people (b) to *be saved* and live for God. He should lead the church in witnessing and see people saved on a regular basis, (c) have regular *baptisms,* so new converts can become faithful disciples. (d) The church should teach correct *doctrine* (beliefs) from the Bible (e) and have *fellowship* opportunities. (f) The church should practice the *Lord's Supper* (breaking bread) as well and (g) encourage and provide opportunities for regular *prayer.* A church with the right leader and people determined to obey God will make a difference forever!

<u>Explanation of Verse 43</u>: This verse refers to the miracles that God allowed the apostles to perform at the beginning of the first church. They are called miracles because these signs and wonders cannot be explained by man and did not happen very often. Miracles are not a requirement of any church. But God can decide to perform miracles any time He chooses. If we have faith in God and it is in His will and timing, we can pray and see miracles too.

<u>Should I expect miracles to be performed by my pastor or staff</u>? Do not expect any pastor or staff person to perform a miracle, even in the name of God. Miracles can happen, but they are not a

normal, regular occurrence. God allows signs and wonders to happen sometimes today as He did then to help people realize that He is the true God. If a miracle ever happens, believers should give God the glory, praise, and honor and not a man or woman.

<u>What do I do if I am concerned about problems with my pastor or my church</u>? Do not be discouraged if your pastor or church is not perfect in every area. There are no faultless churches or flawless leaders. We all should regularly pray for our pastor, staff, and all ministries and leaders in our churches. 1 Timothy 2:1-4 tells us to pray for all people in authority so we can lead peaceable and quiet lives. This will prevent and solve a lot of problems. If you see that your pastor or church is lacking in a specific area, go to Jesus and pray earnestly and consistently about it. It is best for you to not discuss it with other people. Sharing your concerns with others can easily become gossip and can destroy the work of God in your church and in the community. Instead, ask Christ to deal with your pastor and church leaders and control their hearts, minds, and actions, as well as give them wise, humble, and obedient hearts.

Remember that your pastor is just a man and needs compassion like anyone else. He should also be a man of integrity with a good testimony. A pastor is an anointed man of God, called by our Lord to preach His Word and lead the church. In Romans 13:1, it says that God appoints all authority. This tells us that the pastor's position and person must be respected because God put him in his position. God's Word tells us in 1 Chronicles 16:22 – "Do not touch My anointed ones, and do My prophets no harm." If you know for a fact (not hearsay) that your pastor is doing wrong and not willing to repent, then ask the Lord Jesus to work in the situation and for God to do whatever He decides is best for the church. But do not confront and attack your pastor, or handle conflict publicly, as you can bring harm on yourself through God's judgment.

If you become upset about a situation in your church, it is unwise to leave a church hastily. No one should leave out of anger or because of an offense because it is too easy for your emotions to be in control instead of God leading you. Remember, there are two sides to every story and try to think the best of the person. Every church has problems from time to time. Do families have problems too? Yes, and those who are obedient to the Lord Jesus stay committed and work out their difficulties. We also need to stay committed to our extended family – our local church, and give God time to work it out and keep praying! If God leads you to leave your church because of an unfortunate situation, try to wait until you have an attitude of love for all involved and can leave with forgiveness in your heart and in God's timing for you and your family.

Always pray about every decision and make sure you are led by God before joining a particular church. The Lord cares about your choices in this area more than you do. He desires that you choose the best place of worship to serve Him, encourage others, and grow spiritually. God knows the best place for you and your family and the best timing. Consult God first and be led by Him.

Now that you know what qualities to look for in a pastor and a church, you can make sure you choose the best church for you and your family according to the Scriptures..

DAY 4
The Priority of God's House

Memorization and Testimony: Try writing out a memory verse or the Gospel points today.

1. **Hebrews 10:25** – "Not forsaking the assembling of ourselves together, as is the manner of some, but exhorting one another, and so much the more as you see the Day approaching."

2. **Matthew 28:19-20** – "Go therefore and make disciples of all the nations, baptizing them in the name of the Father and of the Son and of the Holy Spirit, teaching them to observe all things that I have commanded you; and lo, I am with you always, even to the end of the age. Amen."

3. **GP7**: Share assurance. (Rom. 10:9-13; Heb. 13:5-6; John 1:12)

4. **GP8**: Share 6 growth steps: 1. Pray daily. 2. Read and obey Bible daily. 3. Go to church weekly. 4. Be baptized. 5. Witness 6. Confess sin. (1 Jn. 1:9; 2 Peter 3:18; 1 Jn. 2:28)

5. **GP9**: Tell someone now what God has done for you. **T**ract, **A**ddress, **P**rayer (Matt. 10:32-33; 1 John 2:22-23)

6. **Share your testimony (and Lead-in and Response questions).** Try to do it today.

Lord, please show me how to be more faithful to You each day and recognize the excuses that the Enemy tries to use to hinder Your best in my life. Help me to develop a greater understanding of the importance of being with You and other Christians in church and small group Bible studies on a regular basis. In Jesus' name, Amen.

Living in Faith

A grandmother, who lived in Tucson, was well known for her faith and her lack of reticence in talking about it. She would go out on the front porch and yell "Praise the Lord!" Her next-door neighbor would shout back, "There ain't no God!" During those days, the grandmother was very poor, so the neighbor decided to prove his point by buying a large bag of groceries and placing it at her door. The next morning, the grandmother went to the porch and seeing the groceries, said, "Praise the Lord!" The neighbor then stepped out from behind a tree and said, "I bought those groceries, and there ain't no God." The grandmother replied, "Lord, You not only sent me food, but You made the devil pay for it."[2]

The Bible says in Proverbs 17:22a, "A merry heart does good like medicine," so we can laugh at this illustration. But we would not really want to call our unsaved neighbors the *devil* as this lady did. We who call ourselves Christians need to possess the qualities of Christ. Many of us are still on the road to learning how to act more like our Father God, and no one will be perfect until we receive our glorified bodies in Heaven. But until we get to heaven, what qualities should we have and look for in other people in a church that claims the name of Christ Jesus? Read the next section to find out.

- **What Qualities Should the <u>People</u> in the Congregation Display**? Read **Acts 2:44-47**.

a) (vs. 44-45) The people were in _____ with one another and had a _____ spirit.

b) (vs. 46) The people wanted to be in the house of God and were there _____, enjoying fellowship with one another, living out the commands of God in their daily lives with each other.

c) (vs. 47) The people _____ God's greatness and had _____ among others.

d) How did God bless the church as a result of their faithfulness? (vs. 47) _____ _____

They did not fight against one another. They thought of each other as family and helped meet one another's needs. (a) The people in the first church in Acts had *unity* and a *giving* spirit. (b) They loved worshiping God with each other so much that they attended *daily*. They made church a daily habit as we do when we eat food each day. (c) The people *praised* God and everyone liked them (had *favor*) because they lived out a loving, truthful testimony, caring enough to win more people to Jesus so often that (d) more *people were being saved daily* and *becoming* disciples and *members*. Are you willing to be this kind of Christian and church member? _____

Now that you know the spiritual qualities to look for in finding the right church, remember that we humans cannot make right decisions without God's wisdom. So make sure you PRAY about the church God wants you to attend and move ahead only when you have an answer from God and He gives you peace about it. When we first become believers, we are excited about going to church and learning all we can about God. But as life goes on, there is the danger of getting a lukewarm heart, then a cold heart. We may be tempted to put other things before our time with the Lord, individually, or in church. We can come up with all kinds of excuses for not going to church or small group Bible study regularly. These excuses are really distractions from the devil. What are some of the excuses or reasons that have kept you out of God's house before?

> We can come up with all kinds of excuses for not going to church or small group Bible study regularly. These excuses are really distractions from the devil.

Check the ones you have struggled with personally:

____ Sleeping in

____ Going on a trip

____ Working so much that I do not take time to go to church each week

____ Being lazy

____ Not committing to make church and small group Bible study a priority

____ Sick, but not contagious, and I would still go to work if I felt the same way

____ Being mad at someone at church

____ Complaining about the way someone handled a situation or treated me at church so I won't go

____ I don't have anything to wear (but I always find something to wear for work)

____ The rest of my family does not attend church and I do not like going alone

____ Not working out transportation (but I work it out to get to my job)

Are any of those excuses worth missing the blessings God had for you that day in church? _____ There may be some conflicts that hinder you from going to church, but as you ask God for wisdom and determine to obey Him, He will bless you for being obedient to worship Him with other believers. We need to be around other believers in worship. It fires us up to have the strength to stay consistent in our walk with God. It is like coals that stay heated when together. We all will bring the warmth of Christ to our world when we stick together and encourage one another.

Are you ever tempted not to attend church? Have other people pressured you to do something else on Sunday morning? Do they act mad if you do not spend time with them during your church times? When you give into temptations, who are you listening to? _____ Do not let anybody keep you from obeying God by not going to church or small group Bible study each week. We are supposed to put God first in our lives, above all other people. If others try to hinder you from church or Bible study, pray for them and treat them with kindness. An ungodly (unsaved) person has no desire to go to church until salvation, so do not expect an unbeliever to want to go. But you can invite the person to go with you. As you pray for him or her and live a godly life before him or her, God can change his or her heart.

> **The small group Bible study is just as important as the worship service. This is the time to get deeper into the Word, form closer friendships, share prayer requests, and be encouraged.**

The small group Bible study is just as important as the worship service. This is the time to get deeper into the Word, form closer friendships, share prayer requests, and be encouraged in many other ways. Have you noticed that the devil fights you harder about going to small group Bible study on Sunday or during the week than he does in attending the worship service sometimes? _____ Could it be when you do not go, you are missing out on Bible knowledge that would have brought victory, friendships that would have brought more joy, and the blessings God would have given you? _____

Some Christians are in homes where the spouse or parent is not a Christian. That is hard, but if you are in that situation, you need to love your unsaved family member and talk with him or her about how important it is to you to go to church. Explain gently to your family member that just as he or she likes to be involved in different sports or hobbies, this is a very important interest of yours. If you agree not to hinder the person from their hobby or sport activity or another interest, then maybe the family member will agree not to hinder you from going to church and small group Bible study. The person might even be willing to go with you sometime. If you show love and respect (and obedience, if a parent) to your unsaved family members, they will most likely not hinder you in attending church. If you do not have transportation or have any other problem that hinders you from getting to church, then call the church or your friends that go there. They should be able to work out a way to help you get there. If you have to work on Sundays, you can try to rearrange your work schedule, trade with someone, or get another job that does not hinder you in obeying God through worship in church. You can usually work it out if you want to badly enough.

- Read **Romans 12:1-2**. What kind of sacrifice are we to be? _____
  _____ What kind of service does God expect us to give Him?
  _____ How are we to be transformed? _____

Remember, we are to be a *living* and *holy sacrifice*, one that is *acceptable to Him*. Obeying God can require some sort of sacrifice while we are alive, but it is always worthwhile. Our love and obedience is the least we can do to show appreciation for all Jesus did for us! It does not show much love in our hearts for God if we do not sacrifice something. Living for Jesus in obedience is our *reasonable service*. In other words, serving our Lord, after all He has done for us, is the least we can do. When we spend time in the Word, either alone or in a church setting, we are in the process of *renewing our mind* by transforming ourselves to have the mind of Christ so we will become more like Christ. Transformation is God's goal for you and me. It happens when we stay under the teaching of the Bible. We simply cannot neglect being in the Word or neglect being with other godly Christians. It will stunt our growth and hinder us from discerning what God's perfect will is in our lives. If we are unable to discern God's will, then we will make the wrong choices and go the wrong path. When we do not make our lives a living sacrifice to God in obedience in any area, we are not only hurting God's heart, but we are hurting our success and affecting others, especially family and friends, whom we influence along life's pathway.

- Read **Hebrews 10:24-25**. What are we not to forsake? _____
  _____

What is one reason it is important to not forsake getting together each week (see verse 24)? ____
_____

We are commanded to be faithful in church and *not forsake that special time each week when we assemble together*. When you go to church to worship God, you are also there to *show others love and good works*, like lending a hand to people who need help. A church is a good place to get our mind off ourselves, and instead start thinking about serving others. We need to be building up the body of Christ through serving in different positions in the church, as well as making friends and encouraging anyone who needs a loving word or smile. If you are not there, then someone's need may not be met spiritually, emotionally, or even physically. You are an important part of the body of Christ. All believers are the body of Christ. We, as the body of Christ, are the real church, not the church building.

Read **1 Corinthians 12:12-26.** Does a body ignore itself or help itself? _____
What would happen if you decided to use only some parts of your body like your eyes, mouth, and ears, but ignored your hands, or arms, or feet? _____

_____

Would you be able to live and function properly as God intended? _____ Just as you naturally *help* all parts of your physical body so you can live life to the fullest, you also need to live and serve in unity with all the body of believers in your church to serve God to the fullest. Then you can impact the world for Jesus Christ as He intended you to do and experience more joy!

Let's suppose you live in unity with everyone at your church, but you do not attend every week. That reminds me of someone who would help the body sometimes, but ignore it at other times. Would your body function properly if that was the case? _____ You cannot serve God through the body of Christ if you are not there consistently. Is it interesting that we can get out of bed for work or school, but when Sunday comes, it is so hard to get up? Why do you think that is true? _____

> **A church is a good place to get our mind off ourselves and instead start thinking about serving others.**

Do you think it is because we have made a commitment to work or to go to school, and there are consequences if we break that commitment? _____ We need to be even more committed to God, do we not? _____ Try going to bed earlier on Saturday night and make Sunday Bible study and church a priority. You will be glad you did. If not, you will be weaker spiritually and not be encouraged. You will not have as many victories over sin. You will not be able to serve God by serving others because you are not there. If you have children in your home, they will also lack in their spiritual growth if you are not the example and leader in taking your family to church and small group Bible study every week.

Another excuse some people have about not attending church is that "I was hurt by someone in church." Do you still go to work or school if someone hurts you? _____ Forgive and move on. Do not let the devil steal your joy by what someone else did to you. The devil makes sure he visits every church. So be prepared to serve instead of pouting, and there will fewer people who are hurt and more who are helped through your kindness and love! Keep going. Be faithful to God. He knows your heart. Worshipping God in church, Sunday Bible study, and spending time with godly people will help you grow stronger and more successful as a Christian and as a person. The devil knows this, so he will try to hinder you from attending through fear, physical weakness, or personal conflicts or other ways. Psalm 84:4 says, "Blessed are those who dwell in Your house; They will still be praising You." God will bless your life when you obey Him in this area.

DAY 5
Exercising My Faith by Taking the First Step

Memorization and Testimony: Try playing one of the memorization games today.

1. **Hebrews 10:25** – "Not forsaking the assembling of ourselves together, as is the manner of some, but exhorting one another, and so much the more as you see the Day approaching."

2. **Matthew 28:19-20** – "Go therefore and make disciples of all the nations, baptizing them in the name of the Father and of the Son and of the Holy Spirit, teaching them to observe all things that I have commanded you; and lo, I am with you always, even to the end of the age. Amen."

3. **GP7**: Share assurance. (Rom. 10:9-13; Heb. 13:5-6; John 1:12)

4. **GP8**: Share 6 growth steps: 1. Pray daily. 2. Read and obey Bible daily. 3. Go to church weekly. 4. Be baptized. 5. Witness 6. Confess Sin. (1 Jn. 1:9; 2 Peter 3:18; 1 Jn. 2:28)

5. **GP9**: Tell someone now what God has done for you. **T**ract, **A**ddress, **P**rayer (Matt. 10:32-33; 1 John 2:22-23)

6. **Share your testimony (and Lead-in and Response questions)** today. God will help you!

_____

Heavenly Father, thank You for never being ashamed of me. Please work in my heart to have right attitudes, learn what You would have me apply to my life, and minister to other people. Please protect me from being tricked by the Enemy, so I can live in victory. In Jesus' name, Amen.

To overcome our enemy, we must be aware of his tricks.

Fill out Tricks 1 and 2:

Trick 1: _____

Trick 2: _____

- **Trick 3: The Enemy will try to Keep Christians from being Baptized.**

When a baby takes his first step, it is so exciting! It means a whole new world of opportunities has opened up for him and his parents. As Christians, the first step we should take in our Christian life is the step of obedience to be baptized. This shows we are not ashamed, but truly on God's team, ready to now walk with Him in our new life in Christ. Though that first step may be scary, it gets easier the more we exercise those new muscles of obedience toward our Heavenly Father. We all know the benefits of physical exercise, but did you know that spiritual exercise is more important than physical exercise? Spiritual exercise will help you and others in a more important way. The Bible says in 1 Timothy 4:8, "For bodily exercise profits a little, but godliness is profitable for all things, having promise of the life that now is and of that which is to come." When we exercise obedience to God, it will not only profit us, but also others forever! There are several spiritual exercises that are extremely important for a healthy, spiritual life, and believer's baptism is one of those exercises. Do you think the devil wants Christians to be obedient to exercise in this area? No, this is one of his main tricks. For Christians to grow spiritually, they must first be baptized, or they are very likely to remain a babe in Christ.

Let's learn about baptism by looking at the Ethiopian eunuch. Read **Acts 8:26-40**. Philip was obedient to the Lord to go and witness to a person God had ready for him.

1. As he arrived in the area, how did he know who he was supposed to talk to? (vs. 29)

   _____

2. What kind of man was God sending him to minister to? (vs. 27) _____

   _____

3. What did Philip say to him? (vs. 30) _____

4. Philip had a sense of urgency. Was he passive and shy, or friendly and aggressive in his approach to tell this man about Jesus? (vs. 30) _____

5. What was the condition before the eunuch could be baptized? (vs. 36-37) _____

   _____

6. What words tell us how he was baptized? (vs. 38-39) _____

   _____

An angel of the Lord told Philip to go south on a specific road. He obeyed. Then the *Spirit of God* told Philip to go near the chariot and overtake it. God sent him to talk to an *Ethiopian eunuch* who had great authority and worked under the Queen of Ethiopia.

The water has no magical powers. It does <u>not</u> wash away one's sins.

Philip then *asked him if he understood what he was reading*. He was *friendly* and *aggressive* in his approach. The eunuch wanted to be baptized, and Philip told him he could be baptized as long as *he believed in Jesus with all his heart*. To sum it up, as you can see, according to Scripture, baptism is an act of going *down* into the water and then he "*came up out of the water*." It is the first step a Christian should take <u>after</u> praying to ask forgiveness of one's sins and believing in the work of Jesus on the cross and His resurrection. The water has no magical powers. It does not wash away one's sins. It is a way that we can show God that we <u>were</u> serious about becoming His children when we were saved, that we are still not ashamed of Him but glad we are a part of His family. Baptism is a physical act, testifying of your new spiritual birth that happened at an earlier date. It means that you are ready to bury your old way of life and start a new life of obeying God. God says the way to blessing is to take this first step of obedience as your gift back to Him. You can show the Lord you are on His team and love Him by identifying with Him in baptism.

7. Read **Mark 16:16.** What will happen to a person who does not believe? _____

    Does it say that we will not be condemned (that means go to hell) if we are not baptized, or not go to hell if we do not believe? _____

    We are *condemned* when we do not get rid of our sin through believing in Jesus. We are <u>not</u> condemned if we are saved, even if we are not baptized. Hell is for those who *do not believe* that Jesus will take away their sin and do not ask Him to do that. Hell was prepared for the devil and his angels. But if you truly believe in Jesus (that means accepting Him as your Savior and Lord), then the natural result is that you will obey God and be baptized. This should happen <u>after</u> you are saved, not before.

    Baptism is like the ring you wear to <u>show</u> you are married. A wedding ring does not <u>make</u> you married. It only shows you are married. Baptism does not make you a Christian. It simply shows you are not ashamed of Christ and you want to obey Him because you are His child.

8. Read **Luke 23:39-43:** It tells what happened to the thief on the cross that believed in Jesus and did not have an opportunity to be baptized. According to this passage, will people who are not able to be baptized but still believe in Jesus through repentance still go to heaven? _____ This is another example that shows baptism does not save a person or take away sins. But someone who is willing to be baptized should show the fruit of his or her salvation by being obedient in this area if at all possible. If you are not baptized, you can still escape hell because it is the belief (which includes repentance) that lets you escape eternal separation from God. The thief on the cross did not have time to be baptized, and Jesus told him after he believed in Him on the cross, "Today you will be with Me in Paradise" (Luke 23:43b). But the thief spoke his belief in front of everyone, and God says in Matthew 10:32, "Therefore whoever confesses Me before men, him I will also confess before My Father who is in heaven." If you are truly a child of God, you will want to be baptized. If you have not been baptized <u>after</u> you accepted Jesus as Savior, then you need to do that very soon. Do not let the devil hinder you in the first step of obeying God. Putting off being baptized can hinder your walk with Jesus and may prevent you from having as many victories in your Christian life.

The Misled Pastor

A teacher was looking for a job in a Christian school. She came across a church and Christian school that wanted to hire her as a teacher. Having never worked for this particular denomination before, she inquired about what they believed just to make sure there would not be any problems with what she taught and what the school wanted her to teach. They told her that it did not matter if her beliefs were different because she was not going to teach Bible anyway. They had a Bible teacher for that. That put up a red flag in her mind since a teacher influences students, and different beliefs could cause conflict later. So she decided to go visit the school and meet a few people so she could find out what they believed. They had not seen her face yet, so she could go and they would not know who she was or why she was asking about their beliefs. She and her husband visited the school, and the person that she ran into was the pastor of the church. She had prayed God would show her what the church believed so she would know how to make the decision, and God had provided the best person to talk to: the pastor. As she asked the pastor some questions about the church's beliefs, they came to the subject of baptism. The pastor used the verses in 1 Peter 3:20-21 out of context (not interpreting it according to the original meaning) and tried to convince her that baptism was part of salvation. The teacher calmly and respectfully asked the pastor questions, but it was aggravating him because he was getting angry as he tried to explain his philosophy. He was not getting anywhere with convincing her because she knew that baptism had nothing to do with saving a person but was only an outward sign of an inward change according to Scripture. She quoted several Scriptures that showed salvation was not by any works, and that if he added baptism to a requirement for salvation, he was making it a work. But instead of listening to the different Scriptures, his mind was closed because he wanted to be right. He was going to preach on baptism that Sunday. She believes God sent her there to make that pastor think and research the Scriptures so he would not mislead his whole congregation. She wondered what the pastor was trusting in for his salvation and prayed for him that he would not teach wrong beliefs to his congregation anymore.

Did you know that there are some preachers and others we may respect that can take Scripture and twist it to make it sound like what they want it to say? The devil did this in the garden with Adam and Eve. We must be careful to look at the context in which the Scripture was written, find out its original meaning in the Greek, Aramaic, or Hebrew, and compare Scripture with other verses in the Bible before we make an assumption on a doctrinal belief.

9. Turn to **1 Peter 3:18-21** and read it to see what the meaning is for this particular passage.

a) Who brings us to God? (vs. 18) _____

b) How does Jesus bring us to God? (vs. 18) _____

c) What does verse 21 explain about baptism? _____

_____

_____

_____

In verse 18, we know that *Jesus Christ* brings us to God, not anything we do. He was put to death on the cross in His flesh, but came back alive through His Spirit. He also had a risen body. We come to God by *believing the Lord Jesus died and came back alive for our sins.* Baptism is *a figure or type which is a* <u>picture</u> *of what salvation is, not that baptism is actual salvation.* In verse 21, the word "flesh" according to *The Strong's Concordance,* is speaking of "the flesh, the body, the flesh denotes mere human nature, the earthly nature of man apart from divine influence, and therefore prone to sin and opposed to God."[3] It explains that *our flesh, meaning our natural capacity to sin, will not be* *cleansed by being baptized. Baptism does <u>not</u> save us by removing any filthy sin from our flesh, but this baptism is a picture of what has happened already in our heart. When we are baptized, we will have a good or clear conscience before God because we know we have obeyed His first command to us after we are* saved from our sins. We are saved through our belief in the resurrection of Jesus Christ for our sins by confessing Jesus as LORD with our mouth as it says in Romans 10:9-13. (Other verses to study on baptism are Romans 6:4; Colossians 2:12; 1 Peter 3:20-21; Mark 16:16; Acts 18:8; Galatians 3:27.)

10. Have you been baptized <u>AFTER</u> you prayed to ask Jesus to be your Lord and save you from your sins? _____ If not, the best time is this next Sunday. Talk with your Bible study leader or pastor, and they will be glad to help you arrange it. Do not listen to the devil and let him keep you from obeying God in this area. You will experience a great joy and peace as you obey Him by being baptized!

If you have already been baptized <u>after</u> you were saved, that is great! You can now know how to explain this important first step to other people as you have opportunities to tell them about Jesus and disciple them in their growth spiritually.

DAY 6

Exercising My Faith by Telling the Good News

<u>Memorization and Testimony</u>: Say five times each and recite to a friend or family member.

1. <u>Hebrews 10:25</u> – "Not forsaking the assembling of ourselves together, as is the manner of some, but exhorting one another, and so much the more as you see the Day approaching."

2. <u>Matthew 28:19-20</u> – "Go therefore and make disciples of all the nations, baptizing them in the name of the Father and of the Son and of the Holy Spirit, teaching them to observe all things that I have commanded you; and lo, I am with you always, even to the end of the age. Amen."

3. <u>GP7</u>: Share assurance. (Rom. 10:9-13; Heb. 13:5-6; John 1:12)

4. <u>GP8</u>: Share 6 growth steps: 1. Pray daily. 2. Read and obey Bible daily. 3. Go to church weekly. 4. Be baptized. 5. Witness 6. Confess sin. (1 Jn. 1:9; 2 Peter 3:18; 1 Jn. 2:28)

5. <u>GP9</u>: Tell someone now what God has done for you. **Tract, Address, Prayer** (Matt. 10:32-33; 1 John 2:22-23)

6. **<u>Share your testimony (and Lead-in and Response questions</u>).** Last chance is today!

Lord Jesus, thank You for being so unselfish and thinking of me daily, especially when You sacrificed Your life for me. Work in my heart today through Your Word. Give me a vision of heaven and hell so I will be used of You to share the Gospel with passion and make disciples of all nations on a regular basis. I know my obedience will affect many lives forever, so help me put aside my fears and trust You with the results. In Jesus' name, Amen.

Be prepared to have victory over the enemy. Let's review: Trick 1 was: The enemy will try to stop you from reading your Bible and praying. Trick 2 was: The enemy will try to keep you out of church and small group Bible study as much as possible.

Fill out Trick 3: _____

Now you are ready for three of the devil's tricks. Be prepared for the next trick. It will not only affect you, but other lives as well!

- **Trick 4: The Enemy will try to Keep You from Telling Others How to be Saved from their Sins**

God's Athlete

If you are an athlete, you have to discipline your body and prepare it for the sport in which you are participating. We must also discipline ourselves with spiritual disciplines to win the Christian race and receive our rewards from God.

1. Read **1 Corinthians 9:24-27**. What prize does God have for you some day if you are faithful to discipline yourself to be an athlete for Him? _____
   An athlete on earth works so hard to receive a medal that will fade away. Will the *imperishable crown* God gives us ever perish or fade away? _____
   Why is it necessary to discipline your body to obey God (see vs. 27)? _____
   _____

If we are not faithful in any area, God could put us on the shelf. That means He would not be able to use us nor help us reach the perfect plan and purpose for our life. *We would be disqualified* in serving Him and not allowed to run in the race or receive the prize. But you do not have to be an athlete to receive a reward. You just need to exercise your faith regularly in the area of evangelism or witnessing. This means to spread the Good News about how to become a Christian, a child of God. Baptism was the first step of obedience. But this next exercise needs to be practiced regularly. It affects many lives forever! Does the devil want you to do this important exercise? _____

> When we neglect this spiritual exercise, our spiritual muscles will become weak. We will also deny ourselves one of the most wonderful experiences on earth: joy!

If you keep going to church, reading the Bible, and praying, but never share with others how to know Christ and how He has changed your life, then you will become a "spiritually fat" Christian. If you are truly a believer, you cannot keep it a secret for long! There are many children of God who are tricked by the devil into being quiet about their faith. But this is not good for us, and will have a worse effect than no physical exercise. When we neglect this spiritual exercise, our spiritual muscles will become weak. We will also deny ourselves one of the most wonderful experiences on earth: joy! We can have joy knowing that we are actually affecting others' lives forever. Your lack of exercise in sharing your faith could actually contribute to someone going in the wrong direction and hinder that person from considering Christ as Savior! But your obedience in giving your testimony with the Gospel and inviting people to come to Jesus could actually cause them to listen to the Holy Spirit working on their heart. Then you can have a part in saving them from hell! Of course, God does the saving, but He allows us to have a part in it. We do not have to be afraid to obey God by exercising in this area. This discipline may be the hardest because we have to overcome the pain of fear. When a person exercises physically, it may cause a little pain. The coach in school used to say, "No pain, no gain!" When your muscles haven't been used a lot, you experience a little pain or soreness. Even better things happen spiritually when you exercise your spiritual muscles. It will be easier to tell others about Jesus the more you do it. You may always be a little bit nervous, because God wants you to depend on Him to help you. But Jesus can truly see if you love Him and other people He loves if you are willing to sacrifice and put aside your fear by telling them about Jesus.

Guilty or Not Guilty

A lady tells of a time when she received a ticket in the mail that said she ran a red light. The camera at the intersection took a picture, and she was fined a certain amount. She had not run that red light to her knowledge. She did not have much money at the time because her husband was out of a job and things were very tight. She needed to go to court and tell them she was not guilty, but she could not afford to get off work, so she wrote a letter and explained the situation. She had gotten caught by the yellow light when she was already in the intersection, and it was too late to stop. Then the traffic stopped in front of her, causing her to sit in the intersection a few seconds after the light had turned red. But she had passed the red light at that point. The light was yellow, and the camera was off in its timing to say she had run a red light. She told the truth and prayed she would not be found guilty. She sent the money in to them just in case, even though she did not know how she would have enough for groceries and gas for a week before getting paid. Then the last week of the month, she received a letter in the mail saying she was found not guilty with her money returned! She was so excited that she told a lot of people in her office about what had happened to her. She had to spread that good news about what God had done for her! She could not keep quiet.

Is that the way we should be excited about being found not guilty by our Judge Jesus? If we truly realize what we have been saved from, then we have got to share it! What will happen if you do not tell your friends and family about Jesus? If they are not saved, they are on their way to eternal separation from God in hell. If you do not care enough to tell them, then who will care as much as you? If you saw a person in a burning house and there was no one else around to save him or her and you already had on fireproof clothing, would you go in and rescue the person? _____ You already have the fireproof clothing on because God sealed you as His child, and you are guaranteed heaven! God will give you the strength to tell others how you came to Christ and how they can also as you surrender to obey Him in this area. Leading people to Jesus is one of the greatest joys you can experience as a Christian!

2. Read **James 5:20.** When you lead someone to know Jesus as Savior from sin, from what can you have a part in rescuing them? _____

If you rescue someone from death on earth, you are considered a great hero. If you help reform a criminal into someone who is a law-abiding citizen, people would probably say you are a miracle worker. But when you help lead someone to Jesus as Savior, you are actually having a part in *saving that person from eternal death and covering a multitude of sins!* Telling others how to go to heaven and be rescued from the punishment for their sins in hell is so much better than saving only a physical life on earth.

The Best Kind of Hero

There is a true story of a man called Frank. (Names have been changed.) He was on drugs and had been involved in immoral behavior to try and find fulfillment, but one day someone told him about Jesus. He accepted Jesus as his Savior from sin, and God helped him have victory! He was able to get off all drugs. He quit getting drunk and did not sleep around with women anymore. God changed him, and he wanted his family to know Jesus too, so they would not go to hell. He told his brother Bobby about Jesus. He said, "Bobby, you are going to hell if you do not repent of your sins!" He said this in love and not in a condemning way. Some people only need to hear of heaven and God's love, but his brother came from a rough background and was involved in many ungodly things. He knew his brother needed to hear about Jesus' love and the place of punishment for sin. Bobby said he saw some really scary things and knew that if he did not accept Jesus, he would be dead and in hell soon. Thank God, he realized his need for Jesus and was saved from his sin!

Bobby's life was changed like his brother's had been transformed. He started studying God's Word and telling everyone he could about Jesus. Some people listened, and some did not. But he continued to be obedient. One day, God called him to be a missionary. He quit his job, and his boss offered him another job which would have made him rich, but he knew God called him to do something more important, so he said, "No thanks." His boss and co-workers thought he was crazy. He left his job and started raising money to be a missionary, reaching people for Jesus. Now he has traveled to other parts of the world and continues to share the Good News of Jesus. What do you think motivates him to tell people about Jesus? It is the love of Jesus and the fact that people could be in a hell of eternal fire forever! He has led thousands of people to Jesus since then. He now teaches many other Christians how to tell their friends and family about Jesus. Those people are going out and telling people how to accept Jesus as their Savior from sin too. Only God knows how many people will be in heaven instead of hell because of Frank and Bobby's obedience to exercise their faith! They are both the best kind of hero because they allowed God's message to be told so Jesus could rescue multitudes forever.

3. What do you think makes a person afraid to tell someone else how to become God's child? Check the ones that apply to you:

_____ Fear of them rejecting me   _____ Fear of losing their friendship

_____ Fear of them rejecting Christ   _____ Do not feel confident to explain salvation

_____ Lack of love for others   _____ Do not want to be made fun of by others

It is normal to be fearful about sharing Christ. Even Paul was fearful, but he overcame it because his love for Jesus was stronger than his fear.

4. Read **1 Corinthians 2:1-5**. What were Paul's weaknesses in sharing the Gospel?

_____

_____

What did he know to share? _____

_____

What way did he overcome his weaknesses to tell others about Jesus? _____

_____

But just like Paul, your flesh has weaknesses such as *not being very good at speaking, not having a lot of wisdom or knowledge, being fearful, trembling, or not being persuasive* like a salesman. We are not able to save anyone. God does the saving. We are just the messengers. All you need to know is the *basic Gospel* (the ABC's) of how you were saved. If you know how you were saved, you know plenty to get started sharing. *You have the Spirit of Christ and His power* in you helping you do it! Who are you thinking of when you checked any of the above reasons: yourself or the one who needs Jesus? _____ When we make excuses for not witnessing to others, we are letting the flesh be in charge instead of the Spirit of God in us, aren't we? _____ The whole idea is to think of the other person's need to escape hell and experience heaven. Do not let the devil trick you into not helping others become a child of God. But what do you do if you do not feel confident in telling others about Jesus? Read below.

5. Read **John 14:26-27**. Who will tell you what to say when you share the Gospel for Jesus? _____. Remember, you have *God's Helper, the Holy Spirit* and His power in you. You are an ambassador for Christ now!

6. **How Do I Share Christ?**

a) Tell them how Jesus saved you. Just tell your story. It is your testimony. You can ask a godly friend to share his testimony with you so you can hear examples of other testimonies. Tell the events leading up to your new life in Christ as well as the date, time, place, people, and details involved. People are interested in a person's personal experience. Notice in Acts 22:1-5 that Paul established a common ground with the people he was talking to before he shared his testimony in verses 6-21. It is a good idea to first start a conversation about other things and find out what similar interests you have. This can open a door to sharing your testimony of how Christ changed your life.

b) Share with someone about Christ indirectly by sharing what God recently did for you. For example, we have shared amazing things God has done for us like providing a car for us in a miraculous way or an answer to prayer. It has really made people think.

c) Invite your friends, family, neighbors, and co-workers to a special event at church. Some people will respond to this invitation if you are consistent to invite them and show you care. But it may be harder for you to get others to come to your church if they are unchurched or of a different belief. But do not fail to keep trying because God cares about these people even more than you do (Acts 16:31).

d) Notice a need they have and take care of it. For example, you could take a dish and visit people when they have a new baby, if there is a death in the family, or if they are in the hospital. You could also cut their grass, offer to pick up their mail, take care of their animals when they are gone, or take them food if they are hungry. Showing God's love will speak for you. This will help you build a relationship with them and provide opportunities for more conversation about God later.

e) <u>Take the opportunity to speak for Christ when the Lord leads you.</u> Share the Gospel message of how to accept Christ. You will know when God is leading you to speak to someone because you will have a tugging, a burden that does not go away easily. You can know that God will prepare a person's heart to be ready for your witness. So start praying for the person, and when God tugs at your heart to speak to others about Christ, know that He will help you say what He wants you to say, and He will use your witness. You can also ask your pastor to schedule witnessing training at your church or take a group to a place where one is scheduled.

f) <u>Get involved in a ministry through your church.</u> God called the church to be the avenue of bringing the Gospel to the world. Pray about a ministry, find out what your gifts, talents, and interests are, get any necessary training, and go for it! God can use you in a mighty way if you let Him.

g) <u>Practice your story of salvation (your testimony) on your own time, or attend the extra sessions offered through this course to help you practice sharing your faith.</u> Remember, we are helping you, so you do not have to be afraid. Do not let fear keep you from having one of the most joyous experiences in the Christian life. Obey God, and get out of your comfort zone and see how God will bless you.

Have you been able to tell anyone lately how to be saved from his or her sins? _____ If not, start today. Do not let the devil trick you from having a part in rescuing others from hell and guiding them to heaven. It will bring you and others more joy than anything else in the world!

Let's review the tricks from our enemy, the devil:

XIII. Form Spiritual Disciplines

A. Trick 1: The Enemy will try to Stop You from Reading Your Bible and Praying
B. Trick 2: The Enemy will try to Keep You out of Church and Small Group Bible Study as much as Possible.
C. Trick 3: The Enemy will try to Keep Christians from being Baptized.
D. Trick 4: The Enemy will try to Keep You from Telling Others How to be Saved from their Sins.

Lord, please reveal to me when I am about to be tricked by sin and the devil. Remind me to read and study Your Word daily and pray to You often throughout each day. Guide me to be faithful to You in church, in small group weekly Bible studies, and regularly keep in fellowship with other Godly believers. Please use me to influence others to be saved and baptized. I need you to give me the strength to be bold with love as I share the Gospel truth with all who need it. I know you will help me keep a commitment to obey You in all these areas so You will be glorified and shine out from my life. Then I can reach the plan You have for me, and so can others You will use me to influence, for Your kingdom! In Jesus' name, Amen.

Conclusion

Way to go! You have finished Part 1 of this Bible study course. It is ending, but you have begun a wonderful relationship with God, your Heavenly Father and Lord. Congratulations on staying faithful to finish this six-chapter course. You are *Starting Out on the Right Foot* in the Christian life. Keep Jesus as number one in your life and continue to consistently incorporate these five important habits for success in all areas of life:

1. **Study God's Word** (your spiritual food) daily and **obey it**.

2. **Pray** to God often each day (your spiritual water).

3. **Attend Church and small group Bible study faithfully** so you can remain strong, be encouraged, serve God, and continue to grow in God's family.

4. **Share the Good News of the Gospel** with other people so they can know Jesus as Savior and Lord.

5. **Disciple others to grow in Jesus**, taking them through this course and other Bible studies so they can also lead people to Jesus as Savior and Lord and disciple them too.

As you commit to God to consistently incorporate the five habits into your life with His help, you will reach God's plan and purpose for your life. You will be able to achieve fulfillment, joy, peace, and see more of your dreams come to reality, and you will impact many lives for eternity!

You are not finished yet. It is only the beginning. Ask your church about Part 2. Continue your exciting journey with God in the next Bible study book:

Following in HIS Steps
Part 2: Walking in the Light

How to Learn More

How Do I Reach God's Plan for Me after Finishing Part 1 of this Bible Study?

Just because this is the end of Part 1 does not mean it is the end of learning and growing. This is only the beginning. Just as a baby drinks his mother's milk and then graduates to solid food, you have learned the milk of the Word. Now you are ready for some real spiritual food. In Part 2, you will start to learn to spiritually eat more on your own. <u>You are not finished with learning the essentials of the Christian life.</u> You need to continue to learn by taking the next Bible study: *Part 2: Walking in the Light.* Check with your teacher and your church to see what date the next Bible study will begin. If your church does not have it scheduled yet, be proactive and ask them to schedule it. Not only will you receive joy, strength, knowledge, and blessings from learning more knowledge of the Word, but you will influence others also. Below are some of the areas you will study in Part 2:

Following in HIS Steps
Part 2: Walking in the Light

* How to Study the Bible on My Own
* Keys to Handling Problems
* Understanding What I Believe and Why
* God's Plan for Relationships and the Family
* Learn How to Win Over Your Enemy, the Devil
* Formula for Successful Christian Living
* Rewards of Serving Christ with my Gifts
* God's Reward for Obedience and Integrity

* How to Get Answers to Prayer
* Getting to Know My Father God
* How to Speak to Others about God
  * Future Events
  * Victory over Sin
  * Priorities for Success
* Understanding My Role in the Church
* Becoming Equipped to Disciple Others

There is so much to learn about living the Christian life! There is so much joy God wants to give you! In order to receive God's best on earth, join a Bible-believing church and study the Bible in a Sunday School or small group class. Listen to Christian radio, read Christian books, and watch Christian T.V. Remember that people on T.V. and radio may or may not be truly Christian, but God will help you discern who is teaching the whole truth and who is not teaching all truth as you spend more time with Him in His Word and spend time around godly believers. Ask your pastor who is teaching correct beliefs in the media. Remember, your new life is the beginning of a new adventure! Don't give up. The Bible says, "I can do all things through Christ who strengthens me" (Phil. 4:13).

APPENDIX A
How to Look up Verses in the Bible

Look in the front of your Bible where it lists the 66 books of the Old and New Testament. It will give them in order as they appear in the Bible with beginning page numbers.

1. All you have to do is know the reference (address) of the verse you want to look up. For example, if you want to look up 1 John 5:13, then you would look for the book of 1 John (First John). There may be more than one book with the same name, so if it has a 1, 2 or 3 in front of it, it is a different book each time.

2. Follow the dots or line on your Bible contents page to see which page the book of 1 John begins.

3. Now that you have found the page, look for the chapter you want, which is chapter 5 in this case. You can follow the guide at the top of the page or flip through the pages and look until you see "Chapter 5."

4. In each chapter are verses. Go down until you see verse 13 in this case, and you have found the exact verse you need.

This course will help you memorize the books of the Bible in order so you can look them up even quicker. Just as you learned the alphabet and later learned to look up words in a dictionary, so you can learn to look up books of the Bible with ease too. Practice with someone who knows how to do this already.

If you do not know the address or reference of the verse, but you know a word or phrase in the verse, then you can look up a certain verse in the concordance of your Bible. If your Bible does not have a concordance or a complete one, then try these other books to look up meanings of words in the Scriptures.

The New Strong's Exhaustive Concordance of the Bible
By James Strong, LL.D., S.T.D.

Vine's Expository Dictionary of Old and New Testament Words
By W.E. Vine

They contain every word in the Bible and its meaning in the original language. These books are a complete concordance for the King James Version of the Bible and some give choices for other versions. Some online sources for Bible study are Biblegateway.com and Blueletterbible.org.

APPENDIX B
Fun Memorizing Ideas

<u>Why do you need to memorize Scripture</u>? There are many reasons. Memorizing verses gives you a sword you can use to fight off the devil's tricks of discouragement, depression, wrong thoughts, and bad habits. You are always ready to evangelize, that is, tell others the Good News of the Gospel so you can lead them to Jesus as Savior and Lord. You can also become better at answering their questions about God. The more verses you learn, the more wisdom you will acquire to make the best decisions in life for you, your children, and others you influence. Choose verses that will encourage you, give joy, and show you the path to victory and right beliefs so you are not swayed to believe wrong doctrine. The Word of God is the greatest treasure you can ever find. If you make memorization of it a life habit, its power will go with you to change your life and others' lives wherever you go.

<u>How do I memorize Bible verses</u>? Start with the Scripture verses and references mentioned in this book. It is a new habit, so start with a small goal and build up. Memorizing all the memory work is an important key in helping you have victory and reaching God's plan for your life. Fun game ideas are below for all ages (especially teens and adults) to try and see how much fun and success you can have memorizing. These ideas will help you learn the memory work much faster.

1. **Learn a verse in a week with <u>Reminder Cards</u>**. Write the verse and reference exactly as it is written from God's Word on a 3 x 5 card in ink. Read it 7 times a day for 7 days. Carry cards with you every place you go. Keep them in your Bible, on your refrigerator, on your mirror, etc. See if you can say a verse to a friend or family member. Keep a record of the verses you memorize and tell your accountability partner. Always memorize the reference/address of the verse (before and after the verse) along with the verse so you will always know where to look it up to show it to others. For example, the address/reference with the verse looks like this:

John 3:16 "For God so loved the world, that He gave His only begotten Son, that whoever believes in him should not perish but have everlasting life." **John 3:16**

2. **Learn a verse with the <u>Erase Game</u>**. Write the verse and reference on a piece of paper lightly in pencil. Check to make sure you wrote it exactly correct from the Word of God. Get an eraser and start erasing one word at a time. The key to making this work is saying the verse each time after you erase a word. Put a light line under where each word was each time it is erased and see if you can remember it. See the example below. (Studies show that writing out words by hand helps our memory better than typing words out on a computer.)

Romans 10:13 "For whoever _____ on the _____ of the LORD shall be _____." Romans 10:13

You have repeated this verse three times already. Erase until there are no words left, only blanks. If you will say a verse 10-15 times, you will pretty well have it memorized. Review the verse daily and weekly and monthly.

Variation 1: Use a marker board, dry erase marker, and an eraser.

Variation 2: Use your phone or computer to write out the verse and reference. As you delete a word, add a line or blank in its place. Make sure to say the verse and reference out loud each time you erase a word and put in a blank.

3. **Learn a verse by playing "Scramble."** Write out the verse and reference on a piece of paper or thicker paper like construction paper or cardstock. Make sure to check that you wrote it exactly. Space the words further apart than normal. Then cut up each word and the reference/address of the verse. Say the verse several times out loud as you put down each word in order on the table. When you think you may know it pretty well, mix up the words all out of order. Then time yourself to see how fast you can put it together correctly. If you need to look at the verse card or your Bible the first couple of times, that is okay. Then advance to practicing putting it together in order on the table without looking at the Bible or your verse card. You can make this a fun competition and help your family members learn it too. Race with each other to see who can put it together the fastest.

4. **Learn a verse by making your own Puzzle with words and pictures.** Write out the verse and reference as you did with the Scramble game. Check to make sure you wrote it correctly. You can draw pictures to help you remember the meaning of the words. Then draw curvy lines with a marker where you will cut it out like a puzzle. It is easier if you draw the marker lines to cut apart only words on each line at a time. Make sure you include the reference/address of the verse. Say the verse several times before cutting it up. Then cut it apart and try to put together the puzzle. Do not be discouraged if you do not get it correct right away. Keep practicing and reading it until you can put the puzzle together without looking at the Bible or verse card. It will be fun when you finish your puzzle.

5. **Learn a verse by Recording yourself on your phone or other device.** Read it correctly from the Bible or verse card, including the reference/address before and after the verse. Then play it back to yourself throughout the day and try to say it perfectly with your recorded voice. Then check yourself later in the week to see if you can say it without listening to the original recording. Record yourself on a second recording. Play it back and check the Bible or verse card as you listen and see what words you missed. Keep practicing until your final recording is correct and you do not have to look at the Bible or verse card. It is fun to accomplish your goal!

APPENDIX C

Memorization for Chapters 1-6: Memory Verses, Books of the Bible, Gospel Points (GP), and Other Reminders

These verses are written out in the *New King James Version* for your convenience. If you had rather learn these verses in a different Bible version, just let your Bible study leader know and recite your memory verses in your favorite version. Please show your Bible version to the person listening to you. Paraphrased Bible versions are not to be substituted for memorization in this Bible study.

**************************** Chapter 1 ****************************

1. **GP1:** God loves you. (John 3:16 and Jeremiah 31:3)
   John 3:16 "For God so loved the world that He gave His only begotten Son, that whoever believes in Him should not perish but have everlasting life."

2. **GP2:** All have sinned. (Romans 3:23; 5:8; 6:23; Luke 13:3; Ephesians 2:8-9)
   Romans 3:23 "For all have sinned and fall short of the glory of God."

3. **Romans 5:8** "But God demonstrates His own love toward us, in that while we were still sinners, Christ died for us."

**************************** Chapter 2 ****************************

1. **GP3:** Jesus, God's Only Son, willingly paid for the punishment of your sin through His death, blood, burial, and coming back alive. (1 Corinthians 15:3-4; Hebrews 9:22b; 1 John 1:7b)
   1 John 1:7b "The blood of Jesus Christ His Son cleanses us from all sin."

2. **GP4:** What would you like for Jesus to do about your sin problem now?
   Romans 10:9 and 13 - "That if you confess with your mouth the Lord Jesus and believe in your heart that God has raised Him from the dead, you will be saved." "For whoever calls on the name of the LORD shall be saved."

3. Complete your **Spiritual Gifts Profile** and turn in at the next meeting. (See Appendix H).

**************************** Chapter 3 ****************************

1. **GP5:** Allow Jesus to save you from your sins and change your life. It is as simple as ABC:
   (Salvation verses: Romans 10:9 and 13 or John 1:12)
   (Changed life: 2 Corinthians 5:17)
   Admit you are a sinner; ask for forgiveness and repent.

Believe Jesus died to pay for your sins and came back alive.

Call on **Jesus'** name (as **Lord**) and tell Him A. and B.

2. <u>GP6</u>: Would you like to pray to God to save you now? *If no, give a tract. If yes, ask questions first with ABC's that cannot be answered with a yes or no. If ready, guide them in prayer including ABC's.

3. <u>2 Corinthians 5:17</u> "Therefore, if anyone is in Christ, he is a new creation, old things have passed away; behold, all things have become new."

4. <u>Testimony worksheet</u> –Fill out testimony worksheet (Appendix F). Hand in this week.

    <u>Books of the Bible</u>: (New Testament) Matthew, Mark, Luke, John, Acts, Romans, 1st and 2nd Corinthians, Galatians…

*************************** Chapter 4 ***************************

1. <u>Ephesians 1:3</u> "Blessed be the God and Father of our Lord Jesus Christ, who has blessed us with every spiritual blessing in the heavenly places in Christ."

2. <u>1 John 5:4</u> "For whatever is born of God overcomes the world. And this is the victory that has overcome the world—our faith."

3. <u>Hebrews 13:5b and 6a</u> "I will never leave you nor forsake you. …The LORD is my helper."

    <u>Books of the Bible:</u> (New Testament continued) Galatians, Ephesians, Philippians, Colossians, 1 and 2 Thessalonians, 1 and 2 Timothy, Titus…

*************************** Chapter 5 ***************************

1. <u>Jeremiah 29:11</u> "For I know the thoughts that I think toward you, says the LORD, thoughts of peace, and not of evil, to give you a future and a hope."

2. <u>Romans 12:1-2</u> "I beseech you therefore, brethren, by the mercies of God, that you present your bodies a living sacrifice, holy, acceptable to God, which is your reasonable service. And do not be conformed to this world, but be transformed by the renewing of your mind, that you may prove what is that good and acceptable and perfect will of God."

3. <u>Testimony </u>– Share your testimony with a friend or family member this week.

    <u>Books of the Bible:</u> (Review by saying Matthew through 1 and 2 Timothy.) Now say … Titus, Philemon, Hebrews, James, 1st and 2nd Peter, 1st and 2nd and 3rd John, Jude, and Revelation! (You are finished with the New Testament!)

**************************** Chapter 6 ***************************

1. <u>Hebrews 10:25</u> – "Not forsaking the assembling of ourselves together, as is the manner of some, but exhorting one another, and so much the more as you see the Day approaching."

2. <u>Matthew 28:19-20</u> – "Go therefore and make disciples of all the nations, baptizing them in the name of the Father and of the Son and of the Holy Spirit, teaching them to observe all things that I have commanded you; and lo, I am with you always, even to the end of the age. Amen."

3. <u>GP7:</u> Share assurance. (Rom. 10:9-13; Heb. 13:5-6; John 1:12)

4. <u>GP8:</u> Share 6 growth steps: 1. Pray daily. 2. Read and obey Bible daily. 3. Go to church weekly. 4. Be Baptized. 5. Witness 6. Confess Sin. (1 Jn. 1:9; 2 Peter 3:18; 1 Jn. 2:28)

5. <u>GP9:</u> Tell someone now what God has done for you. **Tract, Address, Prayer** (Matt. 10:32-33; 1 John 2:22-23)

6. <u>**Share your testimony and Lead-in and Response questions**</u> with a co-worker or neighbor this week.

****

- Copy the Appendix C sheets first, then cut out each chapter section and put the areas to be memorized on your refrigerator or on your mirror, or carry with you to learn throughout your day!

APPENDIX D
Alternate Memorization (NKJV) for Chapters 1-6

If you have already memorized any verses assigned to be memorized, see alternate verses below for you to memorize. Get the alternate verses approved by your teacher beforehand so it will count for your completion of this course. If there are not enough alternate verses for you, ask your teacher for replacements that are not already assigned in Parts 1 and 2. Remember, you still need to memorize and complete all other areas in each chapter (Gospel Points, Books of the Bible, Individual Testimony, and Spiritual Gifts Analysis) for your certificate. There is no alternate memorization for Gospel points or Books of the Bible. These alternate verses can also be used as extra verses to memorize.

Do not memorize any verses below as a replacement unless approved by your teacher.

- You should have recited all other verses in each chapter you are in so far before being allowed to memorize any of these as a replacement.

- Remember that "sin" verses must be replaced with other "sin" verses, and "how to be saved" verses must be replaced with other "how to be saved" verses, and so on.

Chapters 1-6

(1.) God's Love: **Jeremiah 31:3** "The LORD has appeared of old to me, saying: 'Yes, I have loved you with an everlasting love; Therefore with lovingkindness I have drawn you.'"

(2.) All have sinned: **Romans 3:10 and 12c** (10) "As it is written: There is none righteous, no, not one." (12c) "There is none who does good, no, not one."

(3.) Sin's punishment and God's gift: **Romans 6:23** "For the wages of sin is death, but the gift of God is eternal life in Christ Jesus our Lord."

(4.) Repent of sin to avoid hell: **Luke 13:3** "I tell you, no; but unless you repent, you will all likewise perish."

(5.) Salvation – not of works: **Ephesians 2:8-9** "For by grace you have been saved through faith, and that not of yourselves; it is the gift of God, not of works, lest anyone should boast."

(6.) Forgiveness with His blood: **Hebrews 9:22b** "Without shedding of blood there is no remission."

(7.) Blood of Jesus necessary: **Hebrews 9:12** "Not with the blood of goats and calves, but with His own blood He entered the Most Holy Place once for all, having obtained eternal redemption."

(8) <u>The Gospel</u>: **1 Corinthians 15:3b-4** "Christ died for our sins according to the Scriptures, and that He was buried, and that He rose again the third day according to the Scriptures."

(9.) <u>Salvation</u>: **John 1:12** "But as many as received Him, to them He gave the right to become children of God, to those who believe in His name."

(10.) <u>Not of works, but fruit reveals it</u>: **Matthew 7:21** "Not everyone who says to Me, 'Lord, Lord,' shall enter the kingdom of heaven, but he who does the will of My Father in heaven."

APPENDIX E
Bible Study Tips

1. **Start out small.** If you have never had consistent time with God each day, then start out small. Allow 15-30 minutes at first until you have established a habit. You can allow more time if you need it. It is a wonderful thing to spend more time with God. The time will grow as you increase in knowing how to study and pray in a deeper way. These devotions will take an average of 30 minutes a day. You should also allow some time for prayer. It is a good idea to split up the Bible study in your day by allowing 15 minutes in the morning and 15 minutes in the evening at first until you see what works with your schedule.

2. **Do not be frustrated if you do not finish the Bible Study each day.** Just pick up where you left off the day before. Or you may want to catch up at another time or allow more time than 30 minutes. Remember to enjoy your time with God and let Him lead you. This is just a guide to help you if you need it.

3. **Read the actual Word of God.** Always remember to read some Scripture from God's Word about the weekly topic of study and pray to Him each day. Do not use this book only, but always read the actual words of God out of the Holy Bible. The Word of God has the power to change your life. A book like this one is only a guide to help you understand the Scriptures better. The Bible, God's Word, should be the priority of study in any Bible study, not just a book that a person has written.

4. **God's Word is not to be interpreted by anyone's private opinion** (2 Peter 1:20-21). There may be a lot of personal opinions about what God's Word means. If the person or book cannot back up the opinion with the actual words from the Word of God (interpreted accurately according to the original language it was written in) and many verses that validate the person's claim, then you should not listen to that person's interpretation or opinion any longer. It is a false opinion or the same as a lie.

The Bible needs to be studied concerning its meaning in the original languages it was written in. That is why you will see the author tell you what certain words mean "in the Greek" or "in the Hebrew." The Old Testament was originally written mainly in Hebrew and in some Aramaic. The New Testament was originally written in Greek. Since meanings of words change according to the culture and time period, we must go back to the original meanings of words from the original language it was written in so that we can interpret the Word of God accurately today. You also need to look at the context that the passage was written in; that is, look at the verses surrounding the one verse to find out the point God was getting across in that passage.

5. **Scripture, God's Word, <u>never</u> contradicts itself** (1 Timothy 3:16; John 17:17; Psalm 119:140). God's Word, the Bible, is inspired, that is written from God Himself or "God-breathed." It is the truth and it is totally pure. Knowing this, whenever you do not understand something in God's Word, compare Scripture with Scripture. In other words, look up <u>all</u> the Scriptures you can find on a subject, and you will find the truth. Ask your pastor for more resources.

6. **Never listen to anyone who believes it is all right to <u>add</u> words to the Bible or <u>take away</u> from God's Word.** There are people in some churches who do not believe God's Word is <u>all</u> true. They may add to or take away from the Word of God. Those people are false teachers. False teachers mix truth with error and can sneak in any church. Beware of them and stay away from them. (See Prov. 30:6; Rev. 22:19; 2 John 7-11.)

7. **Study by writing down your thoughts.** There are questions about each Scripture and blanks to answer questions according to God's Word. This is very important because it helps you think and pull your answers from God's Word and not just from your opinion. Bible study is not based on opinions or feelings, but on the truth of God's Word. That is the best way to study.

   We suggest you get another notebook to use for your Bible study notes and prayer requests. This can be one or two notebooks. A simple composition notebook will do.

8. **To look up words you do not understand, use the index or concordance of your Bible.** If your Bible does not have one of these, then you may purchase one that has study helps soon. You can find the true meanings of words from the original Hebrew or Greek by purchasing these two books:

(a.) *The New Strong's Exhaustive Concordance of the Bible*, by James Strong, LL.D., S.T.D.

(b.) *Vine's Expository Dictionary of Old and New Testament Words*, written by W. E. Vine.

You can also go online at <u>www.blueletterbible.org</u> if you prefer. It has many versions and helps for Bible study. Ask your pastor which commentaries to read.

You can also search on your <u>smart phone</u> or other devices to find answers to your Bible questions and meanings of words. Keep in contact with your pastor and teachers at church so they can recommend certain web addresses as well as warn you of any sites that do not interpret the Word of God correctly.

9. **Find a Bible that you can read and enjoy that is accurately translated.** The original manuscripts written by God are inspired. Versions of the Bible are not inspired of themselves, but are inspired only because they come from the original manuscripts. There are many Bible versions out there today. Make sure you find a Bible that is accurately translated from the Hebrew and Greek. Most are accurately translated. The King James Bible, the New King James Bible, the New American Standard Bible, the Holman Christian Standard Bible, and many others are known for being accurately translated. Ask your pastor if you are not sure. A New

King James Bible that has a Thompson Chain Reference Guide in it is our personal favorite for in-depth study. There may be other versions you prefer that we have not mentioned, but make sure to get a Bible that is translated according to the criteria mentioned above. (Beware of The New World translation. It is not accurate and is used by the Jehovah Witnesses, a cult.)

Remember that even when you purchase a Bible that is accurately translated, there may be extra notes on the page, either at the bottom or in the middle or on the sides. These may give you greater insight and help you learn more, but <u>remember that those notes are written by man</u> and not by God and could have mistakes in them.

Watch for the word *paraphrased* on the cover. A paraphrased Bible is really an abbreviated commentary, and not an actual Bible. It is a private interpretation to generalize Scripture so people can understand it in today's language. A paraphrase is just like a book that is a guide. It can be helpful, but remember it is <u>not</u> inspired by God and could have errors in it like any other book. It does not translate every word or thought accurately from the Greek, Aramaic, or Hebrew original manuscripts. If you like, you can purchase a paraphrase to read along with your Bible.

10. **Books of the Bible**

If you have not memorized the Books of the Bible in order, then this Bible study course (Part 1 book and Part 2 book) will help you do that in a simple manner. We all need to make sure we memorize the books of the Bible so we can look them up faster. This helps us follow along in church and Sunday School better so we can enjoy learning God's Word and not be behind the teacher or preacher. It also helps you not waste time during your personal Bible study. Look in the front of your Bible for the names of all the books. You will say the first five books of the Bible starting the third week, and the next five books of the Bible the next week, and so on. Simply repeat the names of the books out loud each day several times. You will learn them a lot faster than you think. You may want to write them once during the week. At your Bible study class or small group Bible study, simply recite them to your accountability partner or whoever is helping keep a record on you. Each week you learn some of the books; always repeat the books you memorized from the beginning of this study, so you will learn all 66 books in order in an easy fashion.

11. **Memorize One to Three Verses each Week.**

Study your memory verse by choosing a method in Appendix B. The suggested memory verses for each week are in Appendix C. If you have already memorized the suggested verses, there are alternate verses in Appendix D as well. Choose verses that go with the topic you are studying in that particular chapter.

12. **When you use this material and attend the Bible study sessions, your assigned partner will check off several things over the length of the course:**

a) If you had your <u>daily time with God</u>, finishing a chapter for each week of the course.

b) If you <u>memorized the Books of the Bible</u> (N.T. in Part 1 book; O.T in Part 2 book.)

c) If you are <u>attending Bible study</u> that week.

d) If you filled out the <u>Spiritual Gifts Profile</u> and turned it in (once in 12 weeks).

e) If you <u>memorized the verses and Gospel points</u> for that week.

f) If you filled out your <u>Testimony</u> sheet and shared it during the course.

These assignments are not hard as they are given to you a little at a time with instructions and examples. This will help you establish habits of success. Do not give up. The checking system is meant to cheer you on like a friend would encourage you. Your church or place of meeting may also have certificates and other rewards to encourage everyone toward consistent Bible study, memorization, regular attendance, and other success habits.

APPENDIX F
Individual Testimony Instructions, Worksheets, and Examples

If you are completing this book of Bible study by yourself (without a Bible class), we suggest you find someone at your church such as a church staff member or leader to check over your testimony worksheet. They will be helpful in giving ideas or suggestions after you complete it.

Once you know whether you have a "Timothy" or "Paul" testimony (see examples in this Appendix), be prepared to write your testimony to share with an individual. What is an individual testimony? It is your own new birth story of when and how God changed your life at salvation. It is an opportunity to share the Good News with one person (an individual) and ask a Lead-In question at the end. This question will give you an opportunity to share the Gospel with that person after you share your story.

This is easy to do. To be prepared to give a testimony to an individual or a few people, simply write out the story of your salvation (leaving out the Gospel presentation for now). Your story should only be between 2-3 minutes long.

1. **Read** through the "Paul" or "Timothy" testimony examples for an individual in this Appendix F. Choose to read the one that seems closest to your own experience. A "Timothy" testimony is for people who were saved as a child or young teen. A "Paul" testimony is for late teen or adult conversions.

2. **Write** out your experience of how your life was changed through Jesus on the "Testimony Worksheet for an Individual." This means fill out sections 1-4 on the Testimony Worksheet under the Timothy or Paul worksheets in the back of this book. When you are finished, it should take only 2-3 minutes to tell your testimony. You do not need to be prepared to tell your testimony yet. You will only turn in the written worksheet of your testimony. You will <u>not</u> be expected to tell your testimony orally in front of the Bible study class. Once you complete your written testimony, it will be easier for you to tell your testimony on a regular basis and be a witness for Christ in your daily life.

3. **Practice reading** your testimony worksheet and **telling it out loud** to yourself or to a friend or family member. This is very important to help you evaluate what you need to work on to make it a natural and smooth presentation when you tell it in a real situation.

4. **Remember to bring your testimony worksheet** filled out to your Bible study when the instructor says to turn it in. Your teacher will help you with any questions you may have and give you more ideas. It is simply your story of what happened to you. You will be so excited and more confident in sharing your new birth salvation story after you finish this. You are now on

your way to being used of God to change other people's lives and have a part in bringing them to salvation! You will see how this brings more joy in your life too.

5. **Choose 1 of the lead-in questions** to add to the bottom of your testimony sheet so you can be ready to share the Gospel to an unsaved person when you use it in a real situation.

Sample Lead-In Questions and Response Questions

The questions below are for you to choose to write at the end of your individual testimony worksheet and to start out your Gospel presentation. Choose one of the Lead-In questions (1, 2, 3, or 4), or one suggested by your teacher, and write it on your individual testimony worksheet. Also write the Response question under the Lead-In question on your testimony worksheet. You will find suggested *Salvation Verses and Gospel Points* to lead someone to Christ in Appendix G.

1. **Lead-In Question:** In your opinion, what do you think it takes for a person to have a changed life and go to heaven? **Response question:** *After the answer, you say:* "May I share with you from the Bible how you can have a changed life and go to heaven someday?" *Start sharing salvation verses— the plan of Salvation.*

2. **Lead-In Question:** In your opinion, when you stand before God someday, why should He let you into heaven? **Response question:** *After the answer, you say:* "May I share with you how you can know for sure that God will allow you into heaven according to the Bible?" *Share salvation verses – the plan of Salvation.*

For people claiming to be saved already:

3. **Lead-In Question:** I love to hear other life stories of salvation. Would you share with me your salvation story of your changed life? *After the answer, if it is not a clear testimony that shows the person knows the right way of salvation and is sure that he or she is saved and has evidence of a changed life, then say:*

    Response question: "May I share real quickly why I know God changed my life and I am on my way to heaven according to the Bible, and how you can know for sure too?" *Share salvation verses –the plan of Salvation.*

For people who do not believe in the Bible, heaven, or believe in God yet:

4. **Lead-In Question:** I think it is very interesting to hear other people's beliefs. What are your beliefs about how to have your sins forgiven by God and enter heaven?

After the answer, <u>never</u> be argumentative. Instead, explain this:

    Response question – part A: Since no human has all knowledge, including us, could there be a chance there could be a higher power like God?

Give the person some facts to think about. Example below:

I hope you will think about how my life was changed beyond my control. There are many evidences that the Bible, heaven, and God are real. For example, God recorded over 300+ prophecies that have come true! The chance of just 8 prophecies coming true is only 1 in 10 x17 power (10 with 17 zeros behind it). There is historical and scientific evidence and of course many changed lives like mine!

Response question – part B: Would you like for me to get you some of this evidence to think about? *Jesus made people think by asking them questions. When you ask friendly questions, it can help people eventually realize the truth and come to their own conclusion. Then they will not feel you are pressuring them. It will be their decision.*

Example questions to get people to think:

a)   How do you think the world came into existence?

b)   Where did the explosion (or atoms and molecules) come from?

c)   I have to have a recipe just for a cake or cookies to possibly turn out right. Where do you think the recipe came from for our human DNA to make our complex bodies function so perfectly?

d)   If there is a higher power, who do you think it might be?

e)   Who is Jesus: Teacher, Prophet, Lunatic or God? Why?

f)   What do you think happens after death?

There are many Christian books that can help you know how to explain with evidence that God is real, that the Bible was written by God, and can be trusted to be totally true. Some resources are below:

* *Scientific Facts in the Bible: 100 Reasons to Believe the Bible is Supernatural in Origin*, by Ray Comfort, (Bridge-Logos, 2001).
* *God Doesn't Believe in Atheists: Proof That the Atheist Doesn't Exist*, by Ray Comfort, (Bridge-Logos, 1993, 2003, 2005).
* *The Case for Christ*, by Lee Strobel, (ZONDERVAN, 1998).
* *The Case for Faith, Revised Study Guide, Investigating the Toughest Objections to Christianity*, by Lee Strobel, (ZONDERVAN, 2013).
* *The Case for Easter*, by Lee Strobel, (ZONDERVAN, 2014).
* *Who Made God? And Answers to Over 100 Other Tough Questions of Faith*, by Ravi Zacharias and Norman Geisler, (ZONDERVAN, 2003).

Ask your pastor for suggestions and other resources.

Worksheet for an Individual Testimony

You do not have to tell how to be saved <u>during</u> this testimony unless God leads you to do so. But make sure you share the Gospel at the end, after the Lead-In and Response questions.

Write either: <u>Paul</u> (adult salvation) or <u>Timothy</u> (child salvation) _____

1. **My Name is:** _____ **Time:** _____ minutes

2. **Tell What My Life was like BEFORE Jesus:** *You can give examples of things you were involved in doing and tell how those things or your lifestyle were out of control (but you do not have to be specific). Use some example words below and tell how you had an emptiness, guilt, sadness, depression, bitterness, or loneliness. Tell how you felt rejected, angry, discontented, unfulfilled, fearful, confused, ashamed, with no purpose or direction, or out of control, etc.* _____
   _____
   _____
   _____
   _____
   _____

   Link: But then one day my life changed on the inside because of a new relationship. *Use this link sentence or write your own link sentence here.* _____
   _____

3. **How My Life Has Changed AFTER Starting My Personal Relationship with God:**

   Ideas: Tell the opposite of whatever words you used to describe your old life. For example, you were guilty, but now you are free from guilt. Use words that go with your personal experience such as I have meaning in my life now, a purpose for living, a boldness, joy, courage, confidence, hope, acceptance, new desires to obey God, victories over sin. I am not alone anymore, and have peace, contentment, etc. You can quote a verse about the area that describes your victory if you like. Share victories and your interests, and how God has used them, lessons you have learned, prayers answered, how God provided, convictions you live by now, and the love you have in Jesus, Praise God for what He has done, who He is (attributes of God), etc. <u>You have 2-3 minutes for this whole story</u>. Write this on another piece of paper or use this sheet. _____
   _____
   _____
   _____
   _____
   _____
   _____
   _____
   _____
   _____

Link: My life has been changed from the inside because of my relationship with God and yours can too! *Use this link, or write another one here.* _____

_____

4. **Apply My Testimony Personally by Asking Lead-In and Response Questions:**

    For <u>Unsaved</u> listeners: **Lead-In Question:** _____

    _____

    Response Question: _____

This page intentionally left blank so Testimony worksheet can be taken out to work on and handed in to teacher.

Example of a "Timothy" Individual Testimony

1. **My Name is:** _____ **Time:** 2 minutes

2. **Tell What My Life was Like BEFORE Jesus:** Hello _____. My name is _____. I grew up in a religious home. We went to church, but I did not like going there, except for being around my friends. I remember feeling guilty, even though I was just a child. But I did not want to admit any wrong I had done. I only cared if I did not get caught in it. I felt angry and sad inside, but did not know why. I had loving parents and a good home, but that did not take away my discontent. One day, I listened in church and learned that I was without hope and in danger of hell. I learned that being in a religious environment would not get me to heaven.

   Link: So finally, I was willing to give up having my way and was ready for God to be in charge of my life.

3. **How My Life Has Changed AFTER Starting My Personal Relationship with God:**

   As soon as I gave in and let the LORD Jesus control my life, a weight was lifted off my heart. The date was May 16, 1965. My life changed immediately. I was free of guilt and did not feel angry any more. I remember being so joyful and had a peace I had not known before. I just had to tell someone what had just happened to me. Even though I was a child, I know I had a real change because I can remember it. I have wanted to obey God, and I do not want to sin anymore. I am free! I want to share with others this Good News so they can have a changed life too! God has been faithful and loving, and the One who always keeps His promises and supplies my needs. Even as a child, I knew Jesus was really the true God because He answered my prayers over and over when no one else knew about them. He has taught me lots of lessons as I obeyed Him. When I did wrong, God disciplined me just as a good Father would do. The more I spent time learning the Bible and attending church, the more I learned God's path and purpose for my life. He has blessed me in so many ways. My life has not been perfect, but I know God has been with me and helped me work out my problems. He has protected me from getting involved in drugs, the occult, and wrong friends as I have listened to His advice. I remember the guilt and discontent I had before Jesus changed my life. My life is so much better than it would have been without Him.

   Link: But now I have God with me helping me every day and I know I am going to heaven!

4. **Apply My Testimony to Them Personally by** <u>**Lead-In and Response Questions**</u>**:**

   For <u>Unsaved</u> listeners: **Lead-In Question**: <u>In your opinion, when you stand before God someday, why should He let you into heaven?</u>

   Response Question: *After the answer, say:* "<u>May I share with you how you can know for sure that God will let you into heaven according to the Bible?</u>" *Start sharing salvation verses – the plan of Salvation. See Appendix G for how to lead someone to Christ.*

Example of a "Paul" Individual Testimony

1. **My Name is:** _____ **Time:** 2 ½ minutes

2. **Tell What My Life was Like BEFORE Jesus:** Hello _____. My name is _____.

I grew up in a family that took me to church and made sure all my needs were met. However, I felt like something was missing in my life. To escape this unexplained turmoil, I turned to drugs and women. I thought drugs were a high that would take away the pain, but as soon as I was not high, I felt sad again. I thought women would make me feel loved, but they did not. I was addicted to the high of it all and could not stop. I felt empty and discontented inside, and my life was out of control and I did not know how to change. One evening, I was stopped with a blown-out tail light on my car. Beyond the sight of the police was a bag of illegal drugs. By some miracle, they never saw the drugs. All this did was cause me think that I was larger than life. One dark, rainy night, I was so drunk that I ran over 28 mailboxes and almost killed one of my best friends. Again, I escaped the police and inevitable arrest. This was God's mercy, I would realize later. I was in so many accidents that I have lost count. I should have died many times. Somehow I thought I was cheating death.

Link: However, I did not know that God was about to change my life!

3. **How My Life has Changed AFTER Starting My Personal Relationship with Jesus:**

It was not until August 3, 1983, when I was 23 years old that I heard the Good News about a love I desperately needed! My brother told me I was on my way to a place of eternal torment, a fiery place called hell. That was not good news, but because he told me there was a way of escape, I wanted to hear more, so I ran down to the kitchen to hear him tell me. I had seen a change, a newfound hope, and confidence in my brother that I had never seen before. I wanted what he had. He showed me from the Bible how I could have the peace and contentment he had. I listened to what he said and started a relationship with God who is now my Heavenly Father and Lord of my life. I knew I was cleansed right away. I was not empty or discontented any more. Now I had a purpose and confidence that my life was secure and on the right path. Jesus has given me a home in heaven, freedom, healing, forgiveness, and a new life like I never thought possible. Jesus has blessed me and met all my needs. I quit drugs, alcohol, and immoral behavior. He took away my pain and replaced it with His forgiveness, peace, and perfect love. He totally cleaned up my life when He saved me! Even though I still have some problems, God helps me with any difficulties that come up in my life. He gave me a great family and a chance to serve Him. He answers my prayers and is always faithful to me. I am so blessed to have Jesus as my best friend and Lord!

Link: My life has never been the same again!

4. **Apply My Testimony Personally by Lead-In and Response Questions.**

For <u>Unsaved</u> Listeners: **Lead-In Question:** <u>In your opinion, what do you think it takes for a person to have a changed life and go to heaven</u>?

Response Question: *After the answer, say* "<u>May I share with you from the Bible how you can have a changed life and go to heaven some day</u>?" *See Appendix G to share the Gospel.*

APPENDIX G
Salvation Verses and Gospel Points

Tips for Sharing the Good News of Jesus with Your Personal Testimony:

1. Share your personal testimony.

2. Ask a <u>Lead-In Question</u> and a <u>Response Question</u> to invite someone to learn how to have a changed life through Jesus.

3. Use salvation Bible verses and Gospel Points to share the plan of salvation with the person. This is in the next section. It is a guide that goes well with the Gospel points you have memorized in this course.

4. Show the verses in a Bible and explain each verse.

5. Always ask questions (that cannot be answered with a yes or no) to make sure the person understands (except for invitation question – GP6).

6. To be saved from the punishment of sin, show the person that he or she needs to:

   A. Agree he or she is sinner, be willing to repent, and desire Jesus to be his or her Lord.
   B. Believe Jesus paid for his or her sins with His blood and came back alive.

If the person is ready to be saved and says he or she wants to pray now:

   C. Lead the person in a prayer. (Do NOT pray for the person.) As you guide him or her in prayer, <u>instruct him or her to pray out loud, in his or her own words</u>. This helps you know the person really prayed for salvation, understands what he or she is saying and enables you to give follow-up.

Do not force or push anyone to be saved. The person is ready when he or she understands the salvation ABC's, answers questions with statements (not yes or no answers) and wants to pray to Jesus.

Remember that the prayer does not save the person. It is the repentant, believing heart that God hears. But make sure the person prays with his or her mouth as Romans 10:9-13 tells us.

See more detailed explanation of sharing the Gospel and follow-up in the next section.

Sharing the Gospel

GP = Gospel Point

The Good News is:

<u>GP1</u>: **God loves you** and has a wonderful plan for your life. (Read John 3:16a).
God is Holy, the Creator, Author of the Bible, and is preparing a place for you in Heaven.

The Bad News is:

<u>GP2</u>: **All have sinned.** All people are born sinners, including me and you. (Read Romans 3:23). Have you ever done, said, or thought wrong? *The person must admit he or she is a sinner to be ready to be saved. You can use the 10 Commandments as examples.*
Read Romans 6:23 - Sin must be punished by death, which is eternal separation from God.
Read Ephesians 2:8-9 - No one is good enough to excuse his or her sin.

But God has a marvelous plan so you do not have to be punished for your sins.
Read Romans 5:8 - While you were still a sinner (an enemy), Jesus died for your sins.
<u>GP3</u>: **Jesus, God's only Son, willingly paid for the punishment of your sin through His death. He gave His blood to cleanse you of all sin, was buried for three days, and came back alive!** He went back to heaven and is preparing a place for you to live with Him some day. *Read and explain the* <u>Gospel</u> – 1 Corinthians 15:3-4; <u>Blood</u> - 1 John 1:7b or Hebrews 9:22b; and <u>Jesus is the only way</u> – John 14:6.

Invitation and Decision to Accept Christ

<u>GP4</u>: **What would you like for Jesus to do about your sin problem now?**
Explain how to be saved - Romans 10:9-13; or how to become God's child - John 1:12

<u>GP5</u>: **To allow Jesus to save you from your sins, make you His child, and change your life, it is as simple as ABC: <u>A</u>dmit you are a sinner; ask for forgiveness and repent. <u>B</u>elieve Jesus died to pay for your sins and came back alive. <u>C</u>all on Jesus' name (as Lord) and tell Him A. and B.** *Jesus must be the <u>only</u> God, Savior, and Lord— John 14:6.*

<u>GP6</u>: **Would you like to <u>pray</u> to God to save you now?** *If no, give a tract. If yes, ask questions first about ABC's that cannot be answered with a yes or no. If ready, **guide the person in prayer**, including ABC's. If the person does not get saved, do <u>not</u> give follow-up.*

Follow-Up (for saved persons only)

Explain:
<u>Changed life</u> - 2 Corinthians 5:17, Matthew 7:21 and <u>God's promise</u> - Hebrews 13:5b
<u>GP7</u>: **Share assurance** (only if the person prays for salvation today): Romans 10:9-13 or John 1:12; and Hebrews 13:5-6.
<u>GP8</u>: **Share six growth steps:** <u>Growth</u> - 2 Peter 3:18 /1 John 2:28; <u>Confession of sin</u> - 1 John 1:9.
<u>GP9</u>: **Tell someone now what God has done for you.** (Matthew 10:32-33; or 1 John 2:22-23)
Give <u>T</u>ract; get complete <u>A</u>ddress for follow-up; say Thank you <u>P</u>rayer for salvation.

This page intentionally left blank so Salvation Verses and Gospel Points can be taken out to carry with you.

APPENDIX H
Spiritual Gifts Profile

Name: _____

Answer questions 1-60 honestly. In each row, write number of your answer in one box on right.

# QUESTION	Frequently Enter 3	Sometimes Enter 2	Seldom Enter 1	Never Enter 0
1. A real joy to me is sharing Scriptures with others that need encouragement.				
2. I am able to speak to groups concerning doctrinal truths and have a unique understanding.				
3. I am always giving food, clothing, or other needs to worthy causes.				
4. I am often asked to provide guidance and management for a particular project.				
5. I am outgoing and enjoy meeting new people.				
6. I am willing to be available to follow-up on those I can encourage.				
7. I am willing to share my possessions with others when a job needs to be done.				
8. I believe in giving more than 10% to the Lord's work in the form of special offerings.				
9. I believe prayer works. I have seen many answers.				
10. I seem to have some success in seeing people take positive action after I talk with them.				
11. I can take a complex problem, break it down, and resolve it.				
12. I don't feel imposed on when I need to unexpectedly have someone at my house.				
13. I enjoy doing things for others that frees them up for their work for the Lord.				
14. I enjoy giving suggestions and direction to a group working on a project.				
15. I have a great concern for the spiritual welfare of Christians when they are going through a crisis.				

16. I enjoy making anonymous donations as I share my personal financial resources.				
17. I enjoy opening my home for those who need a place to stay.				
18. I enjoy preparing meals for those less fortunate.				
19. I enjoy sharing Bible truths and seeing Christians grow in the Lord.				
20. I have deep feelings for people who are suffering and those feelings usually prompt me to action.				
21. I enjoy studying the Bible to find practical applications.				
22. I enjoy working on short-term jobs rather than long-term projects.				
23. I enjoy working on the details of a project and organizing people to carry it out.				
24. I give freely and willingly for financial support of Christian endeavors.				
25. I feel comfortable talking with non-Christians about their salvation.				
26. I feel I am able to see God working in someone's life, even when he or she is facing a problem.				
27. I feel I have a unique success in having people listen to me when presenting the Gospel.				
28. I feel the Holy Spirit has spoken to me giving me truths to share with others.				
29. I feel the Lord will provide for my physical necessities when I give to Him sacrificially.				
30. I have a burden for the unsaved and feel God can use me to reach them.				
31. I have a desire to proclaim the Gospel and other Bible truths.				
32. I expect God to answer my prayers according to His perfect will.				
33. I enjoy leading others and offering inspiration in their work for the Lord.				
34. I have a strong desire to offer encouragement to those who are troubled over some matter in their life.				

35. I have always been able to make people feel warm and welcome in my home.				
36. I enjoy working in the background doing things I see needing to be done.				
37. I have had the privilege of delivering messages from God's Word, pointing out Bible truths.				
38. I have seen my dreams come to pass when it seemed there was no way.				
39. I have seen people conquer problems with my guidance over a long period of time.				
40. I have taught a small class in past years and enjoyed it very much.				
41. I have unsaved friends I witness to when possible.				
42. I have witnessed God work a miracle in my life or in another's life.				
43. I have won several people to the Lord in my life.				
44. I seem to have some success in seeing people grow spiritually under my care.				
45. I can see the overall picture of a project when others seem to see only small segments.				
46. I think I can see God's plans fulfilled even before they happen.				
47. I want to be available to do any job or task to be a help at the church.				
48. I would be willing to take the leadership position on a committee in the church.				
49. It seems like people call on me when someone in distress needs help.				
50. It's a real joy to me to work with people for periods of time and see their lives make major changes.				
51. My heart goes out to those without homes.				
52. My home is a place of ministry for my church.				
53. One of the greatest joys I have is sharing my financial and material resources for the Lord.				
54. Others say they have found my explanation of Bible verses enlightening and helpful.				

55. People seem to look to me for leadership when in a group atmosphere.				
56. People tell me it's a real blessing and they learn a lot when I talk about Bible truths.				
57. Pressure doesn't bother me much when working on a project.				
58. The long-term spiritual welfare of people is important to me.				
59. Things I have learned in the Bible burn inside me, making me want to proclaim them to others.				
60. When I speak up, people generally take my advice and follow my guidance.				

Following in HIS Steps
Part 1: Starting Out on the Right Foot©

Spiritual Gifts Profile Scoring Sheet

Do not look at this sheet until <u>AFTER</u> answering questions 1-60 on previous pages. <u>Under</u> each question number, write your numerical score for that question.

(<u>Frequently</u> = 3   <u>Sometimes</u> = 2   <u>Seldom</u> = 1   <u>Never</u> = 0)

When finished, add scores across and enter totals. Talk to a church staff member about your results so you can begin to use your spiritual gifts for the Lord.

					Totals	Gifts
2	28	31	37	59		
						Prophecy
7	13	22	36	47		
						Serving
19	21	40	54	56		
						Teaching
1	10	15	26	34		
						Encouragement
8	16	24	29	53		
						Giving
14	33	48	55	60		
						Leadership
3	18	20	49	51		
						Mercy

9	32	38	42	46		Faith

4	11	23	45	57		Administration

25	27	30	41	43		Evangelism

6	39	44	50	58		Shepherding

5	12	17	35	52		Hospitality

Write the names of the three gifts that scored highest.

First	
Second	
Third	

Endnotes

General References throughout Whole Text:

1 Frank Charles Thompson, *The Thompson Chain-Reference Study Bible* (Thomas Nelson Bibles, A division of Thomas Nelson, Inc., KJV; U.S.A, copyright 1993).

2 Frank Charles Thompson, *The Thompson Chain-Reference Study Bible* (Thomas Nelson Bibles, A division of Thomas Nelson, Inc., NKJV; U.S.A, copyright 1982).

Introduction

1 Mart DeHaan, *Our Daily Bread* ® (Grand Rapids, MI, 2004), Reprinted by permission. All rights reserved, August 18.

Chapter 1: The New Birth Story

1 Billy Graham, Just As I Am: The Autobiography of Billy Graham (New York: Harper Collins, 1999) quoted in "BrainyQuote.com," *Xplore Inc (blog)*, 2017.
   https://www.brainyquote.com/quotes/quotes/b/billygraha150661.html, accessed July 29, 2017.

2 Elizabeth Elliot, *A Chance to Die: The Life and Legacy of Amy Carmichael* (Grand Rapids, MI: Fleming H. Revell, 1987), 19-20.

3 A.C. Dixon, "He Took My Whipping for Me", *Bible Truth Publishers* (blog), 1979-1980,
   http://bibletruthpublishers.com/he-took-my-whipping-for-me/echoes-of-grace-1979-1980-how-great-is-his-beauty/la95573.

4 Billy Graham, *Just As I Am: The Autobiography of Billy Graham* (New York: Harper Collins, 1997), 728.

5 "The Man and the Birds," YouTube video, 4:45, from Paul Harvey: The Rest of the Story Radio, 1965, aired over ABC Radio on December 24, 2004, posted by "Joshua Clemons," December 7, 2009,
   https://www.youtube.com/watch?v=ddai8rkXWRs.

Chapter 2: The Evidences of God's Gift

None

Chapter 3: Just Look at Your Picture (Who I Am in Christ)

1 Corrie ten Boom and John and Elizabeth Sherrill, The Hiding Place, (Old Tappan, N.J.: Fleming H. Revell, 1971), 238.

2 Rick Stanley, *The Touch of Two Kings*, (Haynes and Associates, 1986), 12, 13, 19.

Chapter 4: Birthday Gifts (What I Have in Christ)

1 David B. Guralnik, Webster's New World Dictionary, (The World Publishing Company, 1966), 279.

Chapter 5: God's Wonderful Purpose and Plan for Your Life

1 Charles Frances Hunter, Healing Through Humor (Lake Mary, FL: Creation House Press, 2003), 60.

2 Jim Elliot, "The Journals of Jim Elliot," (Oct. 28, 1949): 1, quoted in Kevin Halloran, *Anchored in Christ* (blog), October 28, 2013, www.kevinhalloran.net/jim-elliot-quote-he-is-no-fool/.

3 Author unknown, "Trusting God: Jenny's Pearl Necklace," *Changing Lives Foundation* (blog), June 29, 2017,
   http://www.drug-addiction-help-now.org/blog/2012/04/trusting-god-jennys-pearl-necklace/.

Chapter 6: Watching Out for the Main Tricks of Your Enemy: Tricks 1-4

1 Ed Stetzer, "Barna: How Many Have a Biblical Worldview?," www.christianitytoday.com, March 9, 2009, www.christianitytoday.com/edstetzer/2009/march/barna-how-many-have-biblical-worldview.html.

2 Charles Frances Hunter, *Healing Through Humor*, (Lake Mary, FL: Creation House Press, 2003), 57.

3 James Strong, LL.D, S.T.D., *The Strong's Exhaustive Concordance* (Nashville, TN: Thomas Nelson Publishers, 1995) 1 Peter 3:21 - "flesh" G4561, www.blueletterbible.org/lang/lexicon/lexicon.cfm?Strongs=G4561&t=NKJV.

Real Life Impact Ministries, Inc.

We are a non-profit ministry in existence since 2001, dedicated to working through the local church to reach the lost and provide resources for discipleship. We have the goal of assisting churches in fulfilling The Great Commission written out in Matthew 28:19-20, which says, "Go therefore and make disciples of all the nations, baptizing them in the name of the Father and of the Son and of the Holy Spirit, teaching them to observe all things that I have commanded you; and lo, I am with you always, even to the end of the age. Amen."

How do we accomplish our goals?

- We provide training for churches in many areas ranging from children to teens and adults.
- Lead outreaches and mission trips in the U.S. and different parts of the world
- Write Bible studies
- Teach and lead seminars and conferences
- Assist churches in growth strategies through *The Reproducer Plan©*

See the information in front of this book to contact us by e-mail or through our website for questions and easy ordering of our materials or to give a tax-deductible donation to help us reach more people for Christ.

Printed in the United States
By Bookmasters